RICHARD SCHLATTER, GENERAL EDITOR

Humanistic Scholarship in America
◄§ THE PRINCETON STUDIES §►

THE COUNCIL OF THE HUMANITIES
WHITNEY J. OATES, CHAIRMAN
PRINCETON UNIVERSITY

ANTHROPOLOGY

Eric R. Wolf

ART AND ARCHAEOLOGY

James S. Ackerman   Rhys Carpenter

CHINESE PAINTING

Wen Fong

CLASSICS

Eric A. Havelock

HISTORY

Felix Gilbert   John Higham
Leonard Krieger

LINGUISTICS

William Haas   Karl D. Uitti
Rulon Wells

LITERATURE

David Daiches   Howard E. Hugo

Their Authors

MODERN AMERICAN CRITICISM
Walter Sutton

MUSICOLOGY
Frank Ll. Harrison   Mantle Hood
Claude V. Palisca

THE ORIGINS OF AMERICAN
HUMANISTIC SCHOLARS
Robert H. Knapp

PHILOSOPHY
Roderick M. Chisholm   Herbert Feigl
William K. Frankena   John Passmore
Manley Thompson

RELIGION
Paul Ramsey, ed.
James Luther Adams   Philip H. Ashby
Robert M. Grant   J. H. Nichols
Harry M. Orlinsky   John E. Smith
Claude Welch

RELIGION, A HUMANISTIC FIELD
Clyde A. Holbrook

The aim of these volumes is to present a critical account of American humanistic scholarship in recent decades. They have been commissioned by the Council of the Humanities, Whitney J. Oates, Chairman, of Princeton University and were made possible by a grant from the Ford Foundation.

—Richard Schlatter, General Editor.

ART AND
ARCHAEOLOGY

❧ ❧

JAMES S. ACKERMAN
RHYS CARPENTER

PRENTICE-HALL, INC.   ENGLEWOOD CLIFFS   NEW JERSEY

PRENTICE-HALL INTERNATIONAL, INC., LONDON
PRENTICE-HALL OF AUSTRALIA, PTY., LTD., SYDNEY
PRENTICE-HALL OF CANADA, LTD., TORONTO
PRENTICE-HALL OF JAPAN, INC., TOKYO

Current printing (last digit):

11   10   9   8   7   6   5   4   3

FOREWORD

What is the purpose of humanistic scholarship? What, in fact, does the humanist scholar do?

The job of the humanist scholar is to organize our huge inheritance of culture, to make the past available to the present, to make the whole of civilization available to men who necessarily live in one small corner for one little stretch of time, and finally to judge, as a critic, the actions of the present by the experience of the past.

The humanist's task is to clear away the obstacles to our understanding of the past, to make our whole cultural heritage —primitive, pre-Columbian, African, Asian, aboriginal, Near Eastern, classical, medieval, European, American, contemporary, and all the rest—accessible to us. He must sift the whole of man's culture again and again, reassessing, reinterpreting, rediscovering, translating into a modern idiom, making available the materials and the blueprints with which his contemporaries can build their own culture, bringing to the center of the stage that which a past generation has judged irrelevant but which is now again usable, sending into storage that which has become, for the moment, too familiar and too habitual to stir our imagination, preserving it for a posterity to which it will once more seem fresh.

The humanist does all this by the exercise of exact scholarship. He must have the erudition of the historian, the critical abilities of the philosopher, the objectivity of the scientist, and the imagination of all three. The scholar who studies the history of science, for example, must combine a knowledge of languages, history, and philosophy with the knowledge of a scientist. And so on with the scholars who study music, art, religion, literature, and all the rest.

The job is, obviously, impossible for any man; and the humanist scholar, knowing he can never attain his true goal, is always tempted to run after wooden idols whose cults are less exacting and which proffer an easy bliss.

Sometimes the humanist is tempted to bypass the rigorous training of the scholar and to wrap himself in the cloak of the sophist. Then he lapses into a painful wooliness and becomes the "literary" sort of humanist whose only accomplishment is a style which achieves the appearance of sublimity at the cost of an actual inanity. His opposite number is the hardheaded humanist who reacts against empty loftiness by becoming a pedant: he devotes himself to antiquarian detail no less trivial than the banalities of some social science or the mere collecting spirit which is sometimes found in the natural sciences. "Physical science can be at least as trivial as any other form of inquiry: but this is less obvious to the outsider because the triviality is concealed in the decent obscurity of a learned language."

Given the magnitude of his task and the impossibility of total perfection, the humanist scholar must, of course, specialize and his works will often be esoteric. But the belief persists that somehow specialization must be converted to generalization if the humanist scholar is to complete his job. Humanist scholars have not solved the problems of excessive specialization and must share the blame for that catastrophe of communication which besets modern learning.

Humanist scholars have been accused of being overly genteel, contemptuous of popular culture, snobbish and antidemocratic after the fashion of their aristocratic Renaissance progenitors, backward looking, hostile to the present, fearful of the future, ignorantly petulant about science, technology, and the Industrial Revolution—"natural Luddites." "It is a sad thought indeed that our civilization has not produced a *New Vision*," a modern technologist complains, "which could guide us into the new 'Golden Age' which has now become physically possible, but only physically. . . . Who is responsible for this tragi-comedy of Man frustrated by success? . . . Who has left Mankind without a vision? The predictable part of the future may be a job for electronic predictors but the part of it which is not predictable, which is largely a matter of free human choice, is not the business of the machines, nor of scientists . . . but it ought to be, as it was in the great epochs of the past, the prerogative of the inspired humanists." (Dennis Gabor, "Inventing the Future," *Encounter,* May 1960, p. 15.)

Scholars in the humanities may modestly reject the suggestion that they can ever be the inspired prophets of a new age. But their scholarship is essential to enable us to distinguish the inspired prophets from the fanatical Pied Pipers.

The Ford Humanities Project under the direction of the Council of the Humanities of Princeton University is looking at American humanistic scholarship of recent decades, describing it, and attempting to sift the imaginative, the original, and the admirable from the pedantic, the conventional, and the superficial.

We have commissioned about a dozen volumes by recognized scholars in each field. These volumes will give us an account of American humanistic scholarship enabling us to see just what that scholarship has contributed to the culture of America and the world.

Art history and archaeology, like musicology, are new among the humanistic disciplines in America and they still speak with something of the foreign accent of the recent immigrant. The task here is not so much to recount the history of past achievements as to consider the critical problems of method confronting the American scholar in disciplines which have only recently been transplanted to our academic groves.

Professor Ackerman and Professor Carpenter are the ideal

authors for the purpose—they are scholars of the highest repute and attainments, they are known for their interest in method, and neither is timid in proposing novel theories for their colleagues to shoot at. This is the stuff of which lively scholarship is made and I am grateful to the two of them for avoiding the platitudes and uninspired dullness which is the besetting sin of so many "projects." Our aim is to stimulate critical discussion about the humanities in America, not to bury them. This volume achieves our aim with brilliance and learning.

Professor Wen Fong's book on *Chinese Painting,* which is concerned with the study of non-Western art, forms a companion to this volume.

RICHARD SCHLATTER
General Editor

CONTENTS

ARCHAEOLOGY

❦

RHYS CARPENTER

PROFESSOR EMERITUS OF
CLASSICAL ARCHAEOLOGY
BRYN MAWR COLLEGE

PREFACE

In this essay I have refrained from listing in detail, or even summarily reviewing, the work of the present generation of American archaeologists in this country and abroad. Various considerations dissuaded me from such a program. Official publications are readily accessible, and the keen popular interest in archaeological discoveries has ensured a wide dissemination of information on their more important content. But this was not the chief reason for my decision not to compile a chronicle of American excavation and archaeological research. The recent revolutionary advance in technical methods of discovery, recovery, and chronological evaluation has so drastically altered the conduct of archaeological investigation, and opened such unexpected vistas for future activity, that it has seemed preferable to devote myself to the contributions that American physical science has been making to archaeological technique and their exploitation by my profession in the field, the laboratory, and the study. In short, my assigned topic of "The American Contribution to Archaeology" has been interpreted to refer more significantly to present and immanently impending achievement than to past accomplishment.

Had the latter been my major concern, I would have given a prominent place to the Oriental Institute of the University of Chicago, whose seemingly unlimited financial resources during several decades, its brilliant staffs of specialists at work in Egypt, the Nearer East, and Iran, its sumptuous and flawless publications, have been epochal. But the earlier activities of the Institute have been expertly chronicled by the late Professor James H. Breasted in his book *The Oriental Institute,* Volume

XII of the University of Chicago Survey (U. of Chicago, 1933); and no verbal commendation of the Institute's subsequent activities can rival the impression to be gained from inspecting its unsurpassable publications of wall paintings from Egyptian tombs and the excavations at Persepolis and Khorsabad.

Another weighty consideration has been a realization that America's past contribution to archaeological excavation and scholarship cannot be properly appreciated except in the context of the great international community of effort so essential to scientific progress. Herein German participation has been especially conspicuous. Some appreciation of its scope may be derived from the summaries contributed by many specialists to the two volumes entitled *Neue deutsche Ausgrabungen,* ed. Gerhart Rodenwaldt (Münster: Aschendorffsche Verlagbuchhandlung, 1930), and *Neue deutsche Ausgrabungen in Mittelmeergebiet und im vorderen Orient* (Berlin: Gebrüder Mann, 1959). Even were these assumed as familiar to the reader, they would have to be supplemented by a far-ranging conspectus of archaeological enterprise by other than German scholars.

For these various reasons I have thought it best to concentrate my interest and the reader's attention on the program presented in this essay, not in depreciation of work already accomplished, but in anticipation of even more remarkable achievement now impending and in part already begun.

INTRODUCTION

As a distinctive scholarly pursuit with an appropriate domain of study and characteristic methods of procedure, modern archaeology can be said to have had its origin in Renaissance Italy as an offshoot of the humanistic enthusiasm for classical antiquity.

Because of this derivation, early archaeological activity was avowedly a subsidiary of classical learning and concerned itself primarily and almost wholly with material remains from Greek and Roman times—visible remnants, in one form or another, of that temporally but not spiritually remote culture whose written monuments were so fervently admired. These written documents had transmitted a remarkably extensive understanding of the classical achievements in poetry, drama, historical narrative, mythology and religious lore, philosophy, mathematics, mechanics, and medicine. It was only natural to anticipate that the same antiquity's other material survivals, when salvaged and assembled and intelligently considered, would illustrate literature with art and yield a knowledge of classical achievement in fields as various (and as appealing to the Italian mind) as sculpture, architecture, painting, coins, engraved gems, figurines, and metalware. But salvaging and assembling were very different activities from intelligently contemplating and interpreting specimens of ancient art. From the very start, accordingly, archaeology was split into a twofold and sharply differentiated set of practices. In one aspect it was devoted to the discovery and assemblage of artistic material, much of which, having been preserved by being hidden underground, required excavation from the soil; in its other aspect it concerned itself with identifying and interpreting and historically interpolating the material so

5

gathered. Archaeological practice has worn, ever since, this Janus mask, having persevered as a technically elaborated industry for delving the earth in search of material objects and at the same time having persisted as a scholarly pursuit for eliciting accurate knowledge about these same objects in the historical setting of the civilization that produced them.

At first—and for a long time thereafter—interest in the recovered specimens of ancient classical art was partly aesthetic and appreciative of their beauty and superior craftsmanship. These were, quite naturally, the aspects that particularly appealed to the practicing sculptors, painters, and silversmiths of the time. This appeal, however, together with the emulative response of the artists of western Europe to its stimulating inspiration, belongs to the history of art rather than to the history of archaeology. The response of the humanists was of another kind. For them the appreciation and evaluation of these reawakened witnesses to classical achievement was largely literary and learned, as they centered their attention on the representational content of classical art as illustrative of the myths and anecdotes and historical allusions already familiar to them from classical literature.

Archaeology thus applied was scarcely distinguishable from antiquarianism, except insofar as the latter dwelt rather on collecting, identifying, and classifying typical specimens whereas archaeology sought a fuller understanding of their cultural setting—an understanding, however, always considered ancillary to literary humanism.

Johann Joachim Winckelmann (1717-68) has frequently—and not inaptly—been called the godfather of this latter type of archaeology. He furthered its renown with an intense and unflagging zeal, enhancing the antiquary's passion for collecting and classifying objects of art with the humanist's enthusiasm for incorporating them in a literary, philosophical, and critically appreciative reconstruction of antiquity.

6

Since Winckelmann's day archaeology has emancipated itself from classical learning. It has evolved from an ancillary to an independent discipline and in much of its procedure has allied itself quite as intimately to science as to literary studies or art history. However much it may still cherish an inherited preference for classical antiquity to the illumination of Greek and Roman artistic practice and the materially detailed illustration of Greek and Roman history, literature, and life, modern archaeology is no longer primarily concerned with the classical past. From a helpful adjunct to the *Litterae Humaniores* of an outmoded university curriculum it has been developed into a ubiquitous discipline for the exploration and consolidation of the cultural history of mankind.

This was a drastic transformation; but it did not occur suddenly. On the contrary, it was a very leisurely development until, in comparatively recent times, the introduction of scientific technological devices hastened the process of emancipation from the tutelage of the antecedent classical world's written chronicle and historically attested culture. It was not any weakening of enthusiasm for Greco-Roman antiquity that was responsible here, but rather the widening of interest attendant on more active excavation that led to ever more extensive exploration and discovery. At first, such exploration was directed toward familiar goals. A continuing yield of ancient marbles from the chambered ruins of Hadrian's villa near Roman Tivoli; a seemingly endless harvest of wall paintings, mosaics, statuary, and household furnishings from easily disinterred Pompeii and not so accessible Herculaneum; and an ever swelling tide of Greek vases and Etruscan jewelry and metalwork from the Tuscan cemeteries—all these encouraged further digging, even while they continued its concentration on classical sites. But later during the nineteenth century, Layard's spectacular trophies from the palace mound of Nineveh; Schliemann's epochal uncovering of the buried kings of preclassical Mycenae in the grave circle within the Lion Gate; the startling confirmation of the (at first discredited) rumor that paintings of animals of scarcely surmisable antiquity existed on the walls and ceilings of limestone caverns in southern France and northern Spain— all these were factors in the conversion of archaeology from a humanistic pursuit into a dynamically active profession.

This varied and spectacular yield from probing and delving in the gathered earth and cluttered rubbish of abandoned sites and long forgotten habitations brought the student forth from his traditional haunts in reading room and museum corridor to the open countryside wherever the search for objects of historic value might lead him. Under his supervision, gangs of native workmen were supplied with picks and shovels, blunt knives and wicker baskets. The great era of excavational archaeology was in full career.

No one had realized, or even imagined, how much of man's past in recoverable material shape still lay underground. All the more remarkable for its formal variety and aesthetic excellence and cultural significance, therefore, was the excavator's contribution to our visual understanding of human art and industry, the revelation that it brought of the possible scope of man's material accomplishment in favored periods of struggle and triumph. As a result, the systematic investigation of ancient sites by organized expeditions under scholarly supervision aroused so much popular interest and won such effective support from learned societies, museums, and other institutions that it seemed as though the term *archaeology* should be redefined as the intelligent art of digging. The typical archaeologist was, first and foremost, an excavator; and beyond challenge, the only reputable chargé d'affaires for organized excavation was this same professional archaeologist.

There was nothing in the definition of his professional behavior to restrict the archaeological excavator to the relics of

Greece and Rome or, for that matter, to the remains of any specific civilization, whether Egypt or Assyria or Etruria. The methods and disciplines that he had been applying to these lands of more immediate historical interest to the western European mind were clearly independent of country, race, or period; possessing universal validity, they were applicable to the material remains of past human cultural activity anywhere and everywhere in the world. On this estimate of its capabilities, archaeology could not fail to become a generic form of intelligent study, in a category apart, but as widely pertinent to things human as were history and sociology. Like these, it could subscribe wholeheartedly to the noble maxim "Nihil humani a me alienum puto."

Consequent on this widening of external reference there had arisen an internal change of emphasis, which entirely revolutionized the digger's attitude toward his work. Excavation of ancient sites had long been practiced, but it had been little better than treasure hunting in its search for buried objects of marketable value or cultured interest or scholarly appeal. It was, of course, not crudely confined (like the search for pirate's buried loot) to recovering precious metal from hordes of minted coin or caches of jeweled ornament. Broken statues, corroded armor and weapons, ceramic sherds and disintegrated bronzes, fragmentary inscriptions were all sought for, along with every other relic of the past that might interest a dealer or tempt a collector or attract scholarly attention. As long as the material object, in and for itself, was the excavator's objective, the manner of its discovery and removal from the soil, the context and setting in which it had survived, the historical implications of its material environment were scantly considered and very perfunctorily recorded. But more intensive exploration, directed to laying bare an abandoned sanctuary or city or other culturally significant site, could not thus confine itself to casual prizes of removable booty. Rather, each find must be viewed as an integral part of a once existing but now imperfectly preserved whole. As such, it must be made to yield all detectable information, not merely about itself but also about the past in which it originated. Even the deposition of sterile soil above it, around it, and beneath it might be a clue to the history of its aboveground preservation and its disappearance underearth. (Paradoxically, even what the excavator did *not* find might constitute a positive acquisition of evidence.) The correct interpretation of stratified deposits for their chronological implications became a vital element in excavational practice. To this end, the accurate measurement and precise recording of depth levels and physical environment of any and every object encountered, however minute and however devoid of intrinsic interest or value, became a standard requirement of professional routine. The potential tedium of such a performance is seldom envisaged by the general public, aware only of its occasional interruption by some more noteworthy find.

These hitherto unformulated considerations, demanding mechanical skill and unlimited patience combined with special aptitude for observation and inference, transformed the technique of archaeological excavation from an irresponsible and haphazard practice into an exacting discipline with established rules of procedure.

Since this manner and method of technical performance was not dependent on any specific type or cultural stage of human material enterprise, nor in any other way obligated to place or period, but was as applicable to an Etruscan or Far Eastern gravemound as to an Attic cemetery, to an Assyrian or Persian palace as to an imperial Roman dwelling, to a Peruvian as to a Mediterranean settlement—archaeological pursuit was finally stripped of its ties to classic humanism. It acquired an unrestrictedly international status, obligated neither to country nor to race, language, or religion. The only restriction upon its field of action was the requirement that it must devote itself to material manifestations of mankind's past cultural activity.

This material restriction deserves emphasis, since it very strictly defines the field and function of archaeological studies. Archaeology's proper domain is the physical remnant of mankind's past handiwork. Natural phenomena and natural productions that do not result from man's own activity do not concern it. Nor can it claim immediate concern with men's mental activities and spiritual interests except insofar as these manifest and embody themselves as material substance. Thus, written records fall within its purview only as physical matter surviving from former times. The archaeologist claims for his professional concern the papyrus or parchment scroll as a physical object surviving from the past and produced by human hands; but he may not properly insist that its meaningful content for the informed reader belongs to his domain. The inscribed stone slab or clay tablet is his trophy; but the information that its lettered symbols may impart is not his own proper prize, since it belongs as intelligible writing to the linguist and grammarian, and as record of action or event to the historian of human affairs. Appropriately, the archaeologist who unearthed the tablet or recovered the scroll may be the one to transcribe its content and present its photographic reproduction to the scholars of language and the compilers of history. But if he does so, it is in his capacity as one skilled to supplement his archaeological activity with the acquired aptitude of the philologist and the trained insight of the historian. Because of this proscribed limitation to material interests, the archaeologist must ally himself with the physical scientist, into whose province he necessarily intrudes; and it is only as he transcends this alliance and consorts with the humanistic disciplines that the archaeologist may attain the rank of humanist.

It is in this manner, by transgressing his purely material function, that the archaeologist takes over the role of antiquary and connoisseur. It is only right and reasonable that the discoverer of a work of art should be accorded the privilege of prior publication of and comment on the find that he naturally considers to be peculiarly his own property. But when he assigns a newly unearthed piece of statuary or an ornamented vase to its period of origin and the workshop in which it was made and when he ventures to credit a particular craftsman with an unsigned work, discoursing further on historic setting and aesthetic worth, he is claiming for himself the extraneous competence of the expert in art history. No doubt, the long enduring intimacy between digger and dealer, between archaeologist and amateur of art, has resulted in a conflation of interest; the excavator has understandably come to hold the conviction that he is competent to evaluate as art whatever art he brings to light.

For much the same reason, the participation of the scholarly humanist in promoting archaeological investigation of the lands toward which his learned interests incline has fostered the recruiting of the corps of excavators from the ranks of scholars. The archaeologists in the field, engaged on Greek or Roman territory, have with very few exceptions been well-informed classicists. The explorers of the Mesopotamian tells (hills or mounds composed of remains of successive settlements) have very generally been conversant with cuneiform. But this genetic link between archaeologist and humanist has steadily weakened during recent years as more specialized training has been demanded of the properly staffed and fully equipped expedition in the field. The draftsmen, architects, photographers, geologists, paleobotanists, physical anthropologists, chemical technicians, and mechanics recruited for excavational fieldwork in Iraq or Iran (to take an instance at random) need know nothing about cuneiform texts, Achaemenian art, Arabic or Persian history, literature, and language, or anything else beyond their professional accomplishments.

The whole concept of archaeological excavation was transformed by its evolution from a more or less haphazard search for buried objects into a skilled undertaking aimed at recovering information bearing on man's cultural antecedents. In order to meet the demands of this altered conception, archaeologists were forced to devise new methods of procedure. Finding themselves confronted with hitherto neglected tasks in the observation, interpretation, and preservation of the material evidence that they uncovered, they were obliged not merely to perfect their technique of digging, but to turn for assistance to scientific workers in many fields. Relying more and more on scientific knowledge and technological method, they amplified and elaborated a comparatively simple pursuit into an amazingly complex intellectual industry. Instead of unearthing statuary, sifting the soil for coins and carved gems, plundering graves of their content of vases and bronze mirrors and clay figurines, removing mosaics from buried floors and salvaging paintings from crumbled plaster walls, archaeologists were engaged in examining and interpreting the delicate and difficult evidence attendant on destruction and survival in complexes as dissimilar as paleolithic caverns, neolithic settlements, Iron Age cemeteries, stratified city mounds, thrice rebuilt temples, devastated and reinhabited towns, disintegrated monuments, abandoned forts, submerged harbors, disused military highways, minute vestiges of previous cultivation of land now desert or resown.

In seeking to cope with this bewildering confusion and its ever varying demands upon the excavator's inventive intelligence applied to locating, identifying, disinterring, recording, preserving, and ultimately publishing in professional manner the incredible accumulations of material evidence, archaeology lost its straightforward simplicity of content and performance. In spreading its interests and elaborating its methodical devices and inviting to its assistance the collaboration of every available correlated scientific process, modern archaeology (in spite of its adherence to a well-defined aim and purpose) has converted itself into a surprisingly complex miscellany of practical expedients, intellectual aptitudes, and borrowed scientific applications. Its objective has not been shifted from the material recovery and interpretative understanding of mankind's past cultural activity; but the means and methods by which it has sought to attain this objective have been as various in type and as discrepant in performance as they have been empiric in application and fluctuant in result. While on one criterion archaeology has remained a stable intellectual pursuit, on another it has been highly unstable as it has evolved from an unschooled and arbitrary enterprise to an exacting and fully systematized practical discipline.

A major topic in this essay will be the evaluation of the American contribution to this technical transformation.

A second topic, and one of even more immediate bearing on the subject of this inquiry, will be the pertinence of this technical expansion of archaeological science to the growth of humanistic study in contemporary American life.

In archaeology, as in many of the sciences, a crucial division may be made between the descriptive and the theoretic level. The former of these concerns itself primarily with typological analysis and comparison; it is chiefly engaged in assembling, assorting chronologically, and systematizing within appropriate categories of classification the physical material under its control. Linnaean botany, comparative zoology, and descriptive geology may be cited as scientific disciplines of this order. In archaeology, excavational expeditions in the field, professional activity in the museum, and scholarly publication of results from either of these two activities have rather closely confined themselves to this analytic-descriptive function. In the modern career of several of the sciences, a comparable collecting and typological ordering of data have constituted an initial phase of development, and synthetic organization and constructive generalization have appeared only later on the scene. Archaeology has exhibited this same pattern of formal growth. There has been an enormous expenditure of individual energy and collective resources on archaeological exploration, systematic excavation, collection and analytic study, directed to salvaging and making accessible to scholars and the interested public a stupendous variety of specimens of the architectural construction, the representational and decorative arts, and the cultural artifacts from every accessible region and distinguishable period of human activity. But there has been rather conspicuously less performance in putting these well-ordered raw materials to more intelligent use. There has been widely lacking any evidence for the entry of archaeological studies upon the more mature phase in which humanistic understanding should supplant technological competence.

The materially practical versus the intellectually speculative orientations that distinguish these two phases are so diverse in nature and make such differing demands upon individual interests, training, and talent that any estimate of the American contribution to the progress of archaeology must take strictly into account which aspect is under consideration. It is very significant that while this country has stood well to the fore in technological advance in archaeological procedure, having shown conspicuous aptitude for devising and putting into operation accessory scientific methods of detection, critical examination, and preservation of material, at the same time it has left no corresponding mark in humanistic studies related to these material results.

In order to make this distinction more apparent, the present inquiry will be divided into two separate and sharply distinguished parts. The first part in three chapters will deal with professional method and technological progress, while the final chapter will consider the humanistic and cultural contribution of contemporary archaeological science.

&§ 2 §&

DISCOVERY

It is a highly peculiar circumstance that so many of the things
that human hands have made do not disappear entirely and forever with the death of their makers but pass beneath the earth's
surface to be safeguarded from nature's and man's destructive
energy. It is this circumstance that makes excavational archaeology possible and ensures it as a profitable pursuit. In comparison with the things that men have continuously held in their
keeping through the centuries—treasures such as the imperial
cameos of the Augustan age of Rome, or the Byzantine *pala
d'oro* in St. Mark's in Venice and the other scattered relics from
the Latin crusade's detestably un-Christian sack of Constantino-
ple—in comparison with these things that men have preserved,
the precious things that they have lost are incomparably more
numerous. Remove from the world's museums those Greek and
Roman statues that have been recovered from time's hiding
places underground and leave on exhibition only those statues
that have always remained aboveground since ancient times,
and the galleries will be all but empty. It is true that many architectural survivals from the past—such as the Romanesque
churches and Gothic cathedrals of western Europe—have been
preserved, but it is also true that man has willfully destroyed
quite as much as he has preserved, despite the religious sanc-
tion that ought to have made such structures immune. Lost, discarded, damaged, ruined, or disturbed—the earth is laden with
man's past; and it is this hidden lode that the archaeologist seeks
to recover, to rehabilitate, and to understand.

Many factors contribute to the determination of a site for archaeological exploration. Because expeditions are generally con-

ceived and planned in the scholar's study or in the committee room of some museum interested in new acquisitions, sites are often chosen on the basis of literary sources and available geographic information. The decision to explore must, of course, be supported by professional opinion and perhaps supplemented by a brief trial probing of the soil—for a chosen site, however promising it may appear to scholars far from the scene of proposed operation, may upon actual examination by archaeologists prove unpromising or unsuitable for exploration.

Frequently, instigation has come from reports of unsought and wholly fortuitous discoveries made by peasants ploughing their fields or hacking in their vineyards, or revealed by the incursion of modern building or engineering projects into areas hitherto unsounded. In deep Mediterranean waters sponge fishers have come upon sunken wrecks of ancient ships laden with plunder from old-time cities and sanctuaries. On the track of the sponge fisher the skin diver of today is inaugurating a wholly new technique of submarine exploration and salvage of antiquities. On land the eloquent testimony of the ubiquitous potsherd shows where human beings once frequented and announces to what period of time they belonged. But since a surface scattering of sherds in itself reveals little, only organized excavation can disclose how much (or at times how little!) of archaeologic interest and historic importance lies deeper underearth.

Here and there, to be sure, less ambiguous indices may be present. In Mediterranean lands a column not yet earthquake-thrown or a spur of masonry from a building otherwise destroyed has projected above the soil; but such conspicuous markers have long been known to everyone and most sites so marked have been dug. In Greece the location of Delphi and Delos and Olympia, of ancient Corinth and Nemea proclaimed themselves to every voyager. In Asia Minor the great buried temples at Didyma and Sardis were marked by random columns still erect, and in numerous other places throughout the Near East the digger has been openly instructed where to set his spade. Today the identification of profitable sites for large-scale archaeological expeditions in these older lands is a less easily solvable problem; and interest is more frequently directed toward intelligent interrogation of recondite evidence on cultural history rather than moved by any expectation of spectacular finds for enriching a museum and enlivening the front pages of the daily press. But elsewhere in the world new sites for profitable excavation are in almost overwhelming supply. The tropical forest growth of Central America has been pretty thoroughly examined, but very inadequately probed by excavation. The high Andes have had considerable attention paid them by virtue of romantic interest in the Incas and, more substantial, in the magnificent megalithic masonry marking their towns, fortresses, and sanctuaries; but the scientific coordination of Andean prehistory demands an enormous amount of excavational control through hundreds of local investigations in the coastal, midland, and high mountain areas of the several Andean countries. Much of Africa and Asia is still, archaeologically considered, completely virgin ground for systematic excavation.

For these projects, as for any and all archaeological fieldwork, whether ambitious with many workmen or modest with but few, backed by abundant or meager financial resources, there is no acknowledged procedure, no set of infallible rules, to guide the prospective excavator, for whom there is in fact no better precept than to follow hard on every clue and make the most of every offered opportunity. Although there is an element of gambler's luck, for good or ill, about every undertaking, not everything is cast on fortune's wheel. The experienced digger becomes wary of choosing an open hilltop for excavating, particularly where ridges are of limestone and the countryside stands denuded; natural forces and local human activity will have conspired to strip it bare. Under contrary conditions, a heavy accumulation of soil below a steep rise or rocky slope favors rapid burial of older levels beneath a protective covering and thus ensures preservation, since deep intrusive fill is the most effective deterrent to depredation by human agency. In general it may be said that the archaeologist aims to dig deeper than the local occupant of the land normally delves. For it is sporadic human interference with older remains that most thwarts the excavator's chances. The reuse of squared blocks from older buildings, the spreading of dismantled mud brick to make agricultural soil, the removal of all metallic objects for their intrinsic value as raw metal without interest in them as artifacts or art, the demolition of foundation walls as obstacles to ploughing and detriment to crops—these are some of the sources of destruction that the excavator dreads to encounter; whereas more instant forces of upheaval and destruction, even when they took the form of enemy sack and pillage, of fire, flood, earthquake, or volcanic eruption, are rated as kindly factors because they tend to preserve what they overwhelm and demolish. The story of Pompeii and Herculaneum is familiar to all; neither site would have rewarded excavation in modern times if Mount Vesuvius had not destroyed them while they were still in their heyday. Indeed, sudden and drastic catastrophe is extremely favorable to prolonged subsoil preservation; a human settlement rapidly destroyed and as promptly evacuated becomes an archaeological document with the supreme merit of being foreclosed to further occupation and exactly dated by its own downfall. For the archaeologist the primary consideration is not so much the degree of ruination or the thoroughness of material destruction as the exposure to subsequent interference by reuse, deportation, or decay. Initial damage—the overthrow of buildings, the breaking of furniture and statuary, the crumbling of painted plaster, the twisting and cracking of metalware, the shattering of pottery and glass—is not irreparable misfortune, since the professional archaeologist is equipped to deal with the relics of destruction. He may even welcome the opportunity to demonstrate the resources of his peculiar skills.

Since there is no golden rule of accepted procedure for determining where and what to dig, the wise may be misled by their own learning. Thus, Sir Mortimer Wheeler, who stands at the top of his profession in England as a teacher of excavational technique, published his reminiscences under the engaging title *Still Digging* (Dutton, 1956) and in the course of his comments on archaeological exploration ventured the verdict that of all the still unexplored sites awaiting excavation the most rewarding would be Balkh in northern Afghanistan. This is the city called Baktra in olden times when Alexander's successors ruled their easternmost kingdom. During and after Persian rule it had been a great center of Zoroastrianism; later it became a crossroad in the spread of Buddhism; and even now it bears witness to its vanished greatness as "Mother of Cities" by a huge circuit of walls with gates and ramparts and a crowning citadel, all in ruin. Yet when, stimulated perhaps by Sir Mortimer's confident appraisal, the museum of the University of Pennsylvania dispatched an experienced excavator to make a season's reconnaissance-in-force, the results were not sufficient to encourage further effort.

It is no doubt true that in the long run of chances the best informed diggers have most often scored successes. The classic illustration of the advantage that trained intelligence enjoys over haphazard seeking is Howard Carter's obstinate decade of searching in the Egyptian Valley of the Kings; he was persuaded that the undiscovered grave of a certain pharaoh lay somewhere hidden among the rifled tombs of the greater rulers of his time. The final confirmation of Carter's belief yielded the most sensational—and on a calmly professional estimate, the most important—archaeological discovery of the twentieth century; and it was due to deliberate, intelligently inspired seeking.

Even so, if one reviews the other notable finds of archaeological treasure made during the four decades since Tutankhamen's tomb was opened in 1922—the early Greek bronze vessels from the graves of Trebenishte in Serbian Macedonia; the unexpectedly rich "Viking" ship-burial from the early seventh century of our era at Sutton Hoo in East Anglia, with its warrior's helmet, sword, and dragonhead shield, its silver vessels, cloisonée ornaments, and gold coin; or, spectacularly apart from any known site or settlement, the gigantic bronze amphora of French Vix, with its cast and chased frieze of men and horses of late-archaic Greek workmanship; and yesteryear's stumbling in the streets of the port of Piraeus on a wholly unsuspected cache of lifesize bronze statues from the heyday of Greek sculptural art—it is clear that chance is still the great excavator. And it must be equally evident that neither chance nor the professional archaeologist can have exhausted time's closely hidden store of secrets and that there must still be thousands of unlocated finds well worth recovery—and no profitable way to find them out.

Ever and again through the ages, man has dreamed of some magic instrument—a ring for his finger, a wand for his hand, a cap for his head—endowed with a power to make its bearer invisible. The archaeologist's daydream is the reverse of this, not to render the visible unseen but to make the unseen visible, so that he may look into the opaque depths of earth and rock and ooze to see what is still lying there. Neither Gyges' Ring nor the Hades Helm ever emerged from the wishful unreality of folktale; but modern science, which has aready materialized so many of mankind's longings, may today do better for the archaeologist's dream. The twitching hazelwand of the waterdowser was at best the instrument of a groping visionary. But now, through earthy covers almost as deep and with far less fallible insight, modern technology has supplied the archaeologist with penetrative vision by lending him the aerial camera's eye, the magnetometer, and the resistivity detector.

Discovery from the Air

Effective archaeological exploration from the sky instead of from the ground remained an unsuspected possibility until the introduction of airplane photography for military purposes suggested its application as an incidental by-product of aerial reconnaissance. As for diagnosis from the surgeon's X-ray films, specialized training and skill are needed for the interpretation of aerial photographs; and this is as true of their application to archaeological prospecting as for their military utilization. In either case, when they are properly interpreted, their yield of information may be remarkable, for war or for the peaceful pursuit of humanistic inquiry.

It may seem strange that objects undiscernible by sight on level ground can be detected by vision from the air, since the eye in either case can behold nothing but the same light reflecting surface of the soil. The explanation is that human seeing is not a mere passive acceptance of reflected light, but an active organization of the retinal field of vision into intelligible form. Significant patterns spread out upon the surface of the earth that do not coalesce intelligibly for piecemeal inspection at close quarters can be organized into coherent identifiable shapes when projected at sufficient distance, as when they are viewed directly down from the air. Even when these patterns are not so insistently apparent that they force themselves on the attention of the aerial observer flying above them, their photographic image, when subjected to experienced scrutiny, will permit their recognition and meaningful interpretation.

Aerially disclosed ground patterns are fortuitous and incoherent when they are the product of purely natural conditions of geologic formation and vegetative growth, without human intrusion; whereas a fully articulated pattern displaying geometric symmetry and repetitional order almost invariably be-

tokens human activity for its creation. Uninhabited and un-
cultivated land is characteristically devoid of the particular types
of pattern that man introduces whenever he ploughs a field,
plants an orchard or vineyard, builds walls or constructs roads
and embankments, inhabits towns for the living or sets out
cemeteries for the dead. Long after these constructions have
fallen into disuse and lapsed into ruin, to become concealed
under accumulated refuse or windblown dust or rainwashed
soil, their buried outlines continue to affect the vegetation
rooted upon them, whether this be chance natural growth or
deliberately sown by human hands. Topsoil lying upon a buried
wall or pavement tends to be shallow and the covering vegetation poorer than that around it; a difference in drainage as well
as in chemical composition influences the superincumbent
growth sufficiently to make a "crop-mark" detectable from the
air under favorable conditions of light and season and time of
day. Although ploughs may run across and above a buried building without interference and grain may be sown and may sprout
and ripen without apparent concern for what may lie beneath,
the character of the soil that rests upon the hidden masonry reflects itself in the stand of grain by some difference in texture,
height, or coloring, becoming as it were a weather-mark of the
otherwise wholly invisible ruin. In opposite effect, an ancient
trench or moat or pit or reservoir tends to fill with deeper alluvial, unstony, and therefore richer soil, so that grass and
bushes and trees grow lustier within its boundaries and once
again the pattern of the submerged relic of human industry is
reconstructed in an outline of altered surface texture. More
striking still is the trace made by a buried causeway such as a
Roman roadbed, which may cross open country for mile upon
mile of straight stretches and harmonious contour curves. Destroyed and abandoned towns leave a vegetation pattern betray-
ing their intersecting streets and crooked lanes and encircling
walls, perhaps the very plans of their buried houses. In this

manner the military air photographs taken at the time of the Allied beachhead landings near Paestum in southern Italy in 1943-45 brought out the grid of the streets and their adjoining blocks of houses for almost the entire city of the Roman period, though these had previously been completely unapparent. Subsequent excavation has confirmed the accuracy of the aerial pictures. Under particularly favorable conditions of season and of light, long disused farmsteads may show the patterns of their crofts and byres and outbuildings, their attendant terraces and kitchen gardens, their cattle-runs and pathways, when viewed from the air under low slanting sunlight—ghostly replicas of otherwise invisible survivals underearth.

Not everything, everywhere, will thus reveal itself to the aerial camera's eyes. In regions of arid desert or shoreland dunes, the drift of sand effectually blankets all beneath it. Certain procedures of agriculture, such as the setting out of new vineyards, the spreading of heavy layers of new soil, the introduction of systems of irrigation, militate against an effective use of aerial photography for archaeological detection.

On the other hand, certain types of antique constructions are especially favorable to discovery from the air. Such are tumulary gravemounds. Even where erosion by weather and removal of the heaped-up earth by human agency have destroyed all projection above the surrounding terrain, the artificial nature of their shape and construction gives them prominence in the black and white of the photographic record.

It hardly needs emphasis that various types of landscape differ very markedly in their yield of interpretable information to aerial prospecting. Much depends on climatological conditions and the particular kind and relative quantity of the archaeological remains that underlie the soil. It is for this reason that, although aerial reconnaissance is a commonplace of military activity in nearly every country, its archaeological application has been much more restricted. British fliers have perhaps taken the lead, largely because the vestiges of Roman and neolithic Britain lend themselves to aerial investigation in a uniquely rewarding manner. The Mediterranean basin and its surrounding lands constitute an almost equally favorable hunting ground, not so much through natural causes of vegetation, soil, and climate as because they have been so long and so eminently civilized. Our own country, in contrast, has less to offer, being temporally short in higher cultures and showing few concentrations of notable remains. There are, to be sure, "innumerable mounds spread over the great expanse of the eastern United States,—shell middens, burial tumuli and ritual mounds, —besides the outlines of ditch-enclosed prehistoric villages"; but there may be a discouraging monotony here, without that diversion of spectacular discovery, the hope of which, despite professed and genuine devotion to the cause of science, smoulders like an undampable *ignis fatuus* in the mind of every digger in the soil. The remarkably successful techniques developed in England have roused American professional interest without stimulating much active emulation. But at least it may be said that the principles of archaeological discovery from the air are well-understood in our country and have had a certain amount of intelligent application to prehistoric research. I cite an example mentioned in the English standard work on aerial archaeology, Jon Bradford's *Ancient Landscapes* (London: G. Bell & Sons, 1957):

> The most remarkable instance of U.S. air archaeology in recent years . . . was the discovery at Poverty Point in northern Louisiana in 1952-53 reported by James A. Ford [in *American Antiquity*, XIX (1954), 282-85]. Surface finds of stone implements had been made at this spot for many years. Nearby is a huge earthen mound, its top 70 feet above the plain; this had been believed natural but drilling has now proved that it is artificial,—as prodigious as Silbury Hill near Avebury [the 130-foot-high prehistoric mound of unknown purpose, in Wilt-

25

shire, England]. Adjacent to this mound, the study of air photos revealed an extraordinary series of earthworks, no less than three-quarters of a mile in diameter, consisting of six concentric banks and ditches,—or rather their remains, for the area is under cultivation. . . . This site had not previously been discovered by observation on the ground simply because it is on too large a scale. The broad low banks have been reduced to a height of 4 to 6 feet, and straight roads through them radiated from the central open space. It seems that the original layout may have been eight-sided and that the Arkansas river channel eroded part of it. The age of the Poverty Point complex is not yet settled, but arguments from geology and radiocarbon dating have suggested a period of 400 B.C. or earlier. . . . One may marvel that so vast an earthwork could be built by peoples of a pre-pottery culture.

Undoubtedly, air reconnaissance will occupy a permanent and very special post in the archaeology of the future. It not only supplements traditional methods of topical research but also supplies evidence not to be derived in any other way from any other source. It may be that considerable experience is required for dealing with certain types of terrain and certain kinds of antique remains, since it is possible to misinterpret the black-and-white photographic record from overhead (much as a surgeon, it is said, must learn to read correctly the X-ray photographs, which cannot lie but may mislead); but there are no difficult tricks or undivulged secrets of the craft other than a discreet choice of the right season of the year and best time of day for successful operation. To quote again from *Ancient Landscapes:* "As with the modern techniques of excavation now spreading round the world, there is no secret in the recipe: there are simply proven methods to be used at the right place and moment."

In Apulia, the southeasternmost province of Italy, air reconnaissance carried out in 1945 disclosed "an unparalleled display of buried sites, extensive, complex, and novel." Subsequent fieldwork and trial excavation, following up the aerial indications, made it evident that air photography had uncovered the ecological topography of the neolithic occupation of this Mediterranean region some four to five thousand years before our time—a field of inquiry hitherto lying comparatively fallow. The airborne discoverers stress the important point that *"no trace of any surface earthworks, of bank or ditch, survived above ground* which could have led to discovery in the absence of the aerial survey." Yet photographs from overhead revealed in terms of "soil-marks" and "crop-marks" the subsoil existence of settlement after settlement, each with its enclosing moats, entrances, and compounds. Streets and houses, since they were of a very primitive nature, had left no mark; but direct excavation could be counted on to reveal their traces and recover samples of their original contents in artifacts. However, without overlooking the necessity of a systematic clearance of a few typical sites by excavation, the novelty in such a survey and the importance for all future archaeological study lies in its transcendence of traditional spade-and-shovel work by substituting for laborious and time consuming piecemeal excavation of restricted extent a comprehensive countrywide survey. Such a survey, by establishing the distribution, size, and formal type of hundreds of contiguous settlements would permit an analysis of the ecological adaptation to physical environment of an entire cultural area during periods on which written history is silent. Success in such an undertaking would raise the status of archaeological study as a branch of reconstitutive cultural history.

The west-central sector of the Italian peninsula was occupied during the first millennium B.C. by a people of non-Latin speech and traditions, known to the Romans as *Tusci* and to us as the Etruscans. Unlike the Greeks and Latins of their time, this people buried its dead under circular conical mounds of earth that ranged from hillocks little more than twenty feet across to impressive structures over a hundred feet in diameter and of correspondingly lofty height. The elemental forces of wind and water, effectively seconded by human interest in securing ready soil for nearby fields, have reduced most of these mounds to level ground, leaving their stone subterranean graverooms unmarked and unnoticeable. More than a century ago, fortuitous discovery of some of these buried tombs by peasants working in fields and vineyards drew widespread attention to the painted frescoes still bright upon their walls and the quantities of Greek vases and metalware often cluttering their floors, with the result that an exceedingly active, distressfully unsystematic, and largely clandestine search was made for hitherto unplundered graves. The middle decades of the nineteenth century are memorable in the annals of unscientific excavation.

Since that time the business of prospecting for Etruscan tombs and disclosing their treasures has passed into more fully legalized and professionally competent hands; and modern technology has substituted the admirable precision of its well-calculated methods for the haphazard and ruthless probing and plundering of earlier generations. Previously, because the Etruscan necropoleis cover thousands of acres, on a scale too large for systematic excavation, and because the leveled circuits of the quondam mounds are seldom distinguishable on the ground, detection of tombs was a matter of probing and bosing and drilling. Bosing—thumping the ground with heavy wooden rammers to test for hollow resonance—and boring into the soil with huge elongated augers to strike sepulchral cover-slabs have ever been the illicit tomb robber's methods for locating sunken graves. (The lovely bronze mirrors with standards cast in the form of standing maidens, which are prized possessions of the world's museums and which are laconically labeled "From Corinth," were secretly extracted from graves located in this manner during the century before Greek governmental intervention became effective.) In Etruria, air photography and diagnosis by periscope have now outmoded this primitive procedure.

Viewed from the air, the leveled surfaces of the demolished mounds reveal themselves at certain seasons of the year by their color—which stands out from that of the surrounding ground surface because of differing soil composition—while at other times the less abundant or more quickly withered growth of grass and weeds or sown crops upon their shallow beds betrays them even more clearly. Because the earthen mounds were raised upon a circular rock-cut foundation within a bounding trench, the washed silt in this narrow exterior cutting has made a perfect circle of deeper soil; the consequent heavier growth of vegetation above the trench exactly defines the contour of the vanished monument.

Aerial military reconnaissance carried out in 1944 over the Maremma (as the coastal district of the ancient Etruscan cities and their cemeteries is called today) supplied a set of photographs. After the war these were about to be destroyed when Jon Bradford, the English specialist in archaeological detection from the air, fortunately had access to them and was able to identify on them the weather-marks of *nearly two thousand* leveled tumuli, the location and very existence of most of which had previously been unknown. Here was, indeed, an embarrassment of riches, since there was no possibility of unearthing so huge a number of underground grave chambers without any prior guarantee that they would be found intact or contain archaeological material of sufficient importance to reward the time, labor, and expense of opening them up. Here again, modern technical invention came to the rescue.

I do not know whether inspiration for present-day techniques was derived from the submarine's periscope peering out of water into air or from the surgeon's exploratory light thrust into bodily cavities to make their interior visible; probably both of these conspired to stimulate someone's imagination and to suggest their application to archaeology. In any case, the laborious task of the grave robber has been lightened by adding camera and flashlight to his probing drill. The exact location of the underground tombs is now fixed by aerial reconnaissance; preliminary tapping and sounding are dispensed with and the drill is without further ado directed to the roof of the invisible tomb chamber. A portable generator, driving the drill electrically, eliminates the tedious labor of the handturned auger. Once the roof has been pierced by the drill,

> a long metal tube containing a camera with flash apparatus is inserted and rotated. Twelve photos at intervals of thirty degrees give a total panorama and show the position of the entrance [to the chamber in the heart of the tumulus] and whether the tomb contains grave-goods or has wall-paintings. . . . At Monte Abetone [the less well-known of the two necropoleis of Caere] as many as forty tombs were examined in twelve days.

Since the above passage from Bradford's *Ancient Landscapes* was written, the new method has been extensively applied by the Italian Service of Antiquities and has been repaid by remarkable results. The Etruscan tombs can no longer conceal their contents.

The characteristic construction within a rock-cut girdle trench, together with favorable local conditions of soil and vegetation, make the Etruscan mounds an almost unparalleled target for aerial photographic detection. Yet they are not altogether unique in their kind. Similar burial customs have been practiced elsewhere under comparable local conditions of climate and soil, notably in the Anatolian hinterland from which (according to the most probable solution to a highly involved controversy) the Etruscan migration originated. There, in the interior of Turkey some seventy miles west of the modern capital of Angora, air photographs of the site of the ancient Phrygian capital city of Gordion bear striking resemblance to those of Etruscan cemetery sites. Adjoining the large flat-topped tell of the city, nearly a hundred tumuli dot the plain. Unlike the Etruscan mounds, a less assiduous pursuit of agriculture in modern times has spared most of the Gordion landmarks from demolition, so that they remain discernible without further guidance. In consequence there is here less opportunity than in Etruria for extensive new discovery by aerial reconnaissance. Neither has the device of diagnosis by photo-periscope as yet been applied to test unopened tombs for their surviving content. Instead, penetration of several of the more conspicuous mounds —including the giant tumulus ascribed to the far from legendary King Midas—has been accomplished by normal processes of excavation, with spectacular yield of old Phrygian metalware and wooden inlay. Radioactive carbon analysis performed in Philadelphia at the physical laboratory of the University of Pennsylvania has largely confirmed the chronology assumed on historical and archaeological grounds. The great city mound itself had long been familiar to the lettered and the unlettered passerby alike and had been correctly identified by the former as Phrygian Gordion; but it was not until methodical and large-scale excavation was undertaken by Dr. Rodney Young on behalf of the University Museum of the University of Pennsylvania that there was any suspicion of the existence within the tell of walls and gateways and building foundations more impressive and in much better preservation than those of Troy-Hissarlik made famous by Schliemann and Doerpfeld in the latter decades of the nineteenth century.

Other Methods of Detection

It cannot be claimed that the above-mentioned devices for peering into the earth have succeeded in making its heavy cover of concealment everywhere transparent to archaeological vision. Although certain types of graves can be made to give up their secret, there remains underearth and underwater a vast store of material evidence of antiquity, whose volume and value no man now living can pretend to know. Pre-eminent among these hidden attestations to man's past achievements are the works of art —the beaten and chased metalwork in gold and silver and copper and bronze, the carved marbles and cut gems, to name only the less perishable items in the category. Where these have escaped destruction or discovery, they lie for the most part much less than "full fathoms five" beneath the surface of the soil; yet neither archaeologist nor man of science has yet thought of any method for discovering where they lurk or seeing what they are. Apart from its crystalline structure marble does not differ in any chemical or physical property from ordinary limestone. It is therefore hardly to be anticipated that, in a countryside as predominant in limestone as the lands of the Mediterranean basin, marble statuary lying underearth can be differentiated from its environment by any mechanical or physical device. But it might be imagined that metalware should be detectable amid a setting as chemically alien to it as clay or humus or detritus. An ordinary mine detector might seem to the layman sufficiently sensitive to isolated metal in the soil to be responsive to bronze statues or caches of metalware or even hordes of buried coins. But an experienced physicist has issued the discouraging verdict that the sensitivity of the usual mine detector "falls off rapidly with depth, roughly as the sixth power" of the intervening distance, even though he grudgingly grants that large metallic objects might be detectable where the covering of soil did not exceed one foot. However this may be, there are some authentic instances of archaeologically important metalwork located by such means. More immediate hope—albeit with distinctly restricted relevance—is held out for the device known as the magnetometer.

In a later section of this report, attention will be directed to the property called remanent magnetism, which is characteristic of baked clay as a result of its subjection to intense heat in the kiln. The particles of oxidized iron present in the clay, having freely oriented themselves (like miniature compass needles) to the earth's magnetic field while the kiln was hot, remain as it were frozen in position after the kiln has cooled, without responding to subsequent shifts of direction in the earth's magnetic lines of force. They therefore constitute a fossilized record of a past magnetic state of the earth; and this will almost inevitably disagree with present magnetic conditions. This disaccord—or, as it is called, magnetic anomaly—produces an extremely minute, yet measurable, local disturbance in the surrounding magnetic field. A portable magnetometer, when brought into proximity, will report this disturbance and thereby advise the operator of the existence of a source of remanent magnetism in his immediate neighborhood. He may suspect this disturbance to be caused by the presence of some form of previously baked clay surviving in concentration in undisturbed position. Loosely scattered potsherds will not record themselves in sufficient intensity to be detected, especially as their fortuitous orientations will combine to cancel out any magnetic influence that they might possess. But a solid clay mass of any considerable size, such as a dismantled pottery kiln or the disused clay hearth of a destroyed house or (under certain circumstances) a brick foundation wall will cause an appreciable response on the dials of the magnetometer.

Magnetic location (as this process of detection has been named) necessarily possesses an extremely limited range of usefulness, but it works very efficiently for the restricted class of objects toward which it may be directed. Rather unexpectedly, its applicability has been extended by the discovery, when magnetic surveying was undertaken in England, that the magnetometer gives characteristic anomaly readings when operated above filled-in pits marking holes in the ground once dug as depositories for food or disposal of refuse, provided that the pits have a strong humus content or have been subject at some time to fire. Since these conditions are almost certain to be the result of human activity, pits evoking a response on the magnetometer can be presumed relevant to archaeological interests. Less concentrated fills, such as those of ancient ditches or sunken roads, have also on occasion been detected by this method. But the device, ingenious as it is, suffers from the handicap that the magnetometer is extremely susceptible to the presence of iron in the soil; and an object as irrelevant to archaeological exploration as a buried horseshoe or a length of discarded iron pipe may excite it more intensively than an entire buried settlement from an earlier age from which iron is unlikely to have survived!

An associated device for subsoil detection, which has been extensively utilized in geological survey work during the past half century, has recently been diverted to archaeological service. A pair of metal probes is thrust into the soil at a convenient distance apart and an electrical current is set in motion to create a circuit through them. Since the return is grounded and consequently impeded if it has to pass through material of feeble conductivity and since rock and stone possess a very high resistivity to electricity in comparison with loose earth and soil, obstacles such as buried masonry and built-up roadbeds intervening between the terminal probes are immediately detectable. Any considerable moisture in the soil, however, since it markedly reduces resistivity, may be more than merely inconvenient and may even annul any effective application of "resistivity surveying."

34

There is still another method, widely used in geologic work, that might be diverted to archaeological prospecting. It works on the principle that fairly low-frequency electromagnetic waves (down to about 500 cycles per second) can be made to record themselves through the subsoil. A transmitter coil is carried by one operator, while a second operator holds a receiver coil several hundred feet away. Any variation in the phase and amplitude of the signal picked up by the receiver implies a variation in the resistivity of the substrata, presumably due to the presence of ore bodies. This device should be capable of reporting random metallic features within a few inches of the surface and metal objects of appreciable size at greater depth.

In 1962 these various devices for subsoil archaeological detection were rather thoroughly tested by an American expedition—under the technical control of Dr. Elizabeth K. Ralph of the Applied Science Center for Archaeology of the Pennsylvania University Museum—working across the site of the vanished Greek town of Sybaris in southern Italy. Although these tests were rewarding, the results tended to confirm previously formed opinion that, as contrasted with the direct and widespread vision of the airborne camera, magnetic and resistivity detection of buried antiquities must be rated as extremely tedious and, unless skillfully performed, highly uncertain methods of subsoil detection. And all such scientific aids, whether operated from the air or on the surface of the earth, are limited by very specific restraints on their utility. Modern science has still to invent a magic means of vision to make silt and soil and rock transparent and their hidden material content visible. Whether science will succeed in thus playing genie to Aladdin in his search for treasure is something that only science can determine. But it is no hazardous guess to assert that, if science succeeds, Aladdin will feel disillusioned with his gift of power. The archaeologist is the lineal descendant of the tomb robber and the treasure hunter; and it is no disrespect to his more serious purposes to claim that in the soul of every excavator there is something of the incorrigible gambler. Chance and Lady Luck are his secret deities; and the possibility of some most improbable success is his unflagging incentive to further effort. To know the entire outcome beforehand would be to rob the enterprise of much of its zest.

Whatever may eventuate, the professional excavator will not refuse to avail himself of the assistance that science may provide for locating sites with sure promise of success in digging. In the past such extraneous aid was not so important. The major expeditions were directed toward sites whose importance was attested by historical record and whose location could be determined by mere inspection or simple trial trenching. Inevitably, such items have been removed, one by one, from the waiting list of attractive opportunities. In Greek lands, Troy and Mycenae and Tiryns and Cretan Knossos were familiar from epic memories; among the great classical cities, Athens and Sparta and Corinth and Argos left only Thebes demonstrably unprofitable to digging; among the great gathering places, Olympia and Delphi and Delos and Eleusis could not be mistaken or left unsearched; there were other temple ruins to be probed and cleared, but most of these announced themselves by their still visible remains. Attention was directed to Macedonian Olynthos by its celebrity in literature, and to Corinthian Perachora by its surface litter of sherds. Today it is no longer an easy matter to fix upon a repaying site in Greece for a large-scale excavation. Similarly, in Egypt there are few important unexploited sites save those that the risen water table of the Delta has made unreachable. In Mesopotamia, Ur and Babylon and Assur were landmarks that encouraged the digging of other conspicuous tells. In Iran, Persepolis and Susa have been dug (but here in the lands east of the Tigris there are still obvious opportunities). Although there are many less frequented regions as yet unexploited by systematic archaeological research, toward which major expeditions still may be profitably directed, in the more familiar archaeological homeland of Europe and the Mediterranean basin it is no longer so readily apparent where greatly rewarding digging may be done. In this connection aerial photographic reconnaissance should prove of the greatest service by scanning large areas with remarkably complete coverage of their surface and supplying pertinent information wholly inaccessible to the earthbound prospector. Yet though much is thus revealed, much more must remain forever concealed from the aerial camera's eye.

Nonetheless, because it is true that the peasant farmer's and the building constructor's and the utility engineer's casual discovery of antiquities continues to rival the best informed accomplishment of the professional excavator, and because there can be no doubt that enormous quantities of valuable material must still lie underearth awaiting discovery, it might be presumed that there is still a marvelous opportunity for science's new devices to achieve detection and to play a major role in the archaeological strategy of the future by scanning the less propitious places and locating the unexpected in its hitherto secure concealment. But the difficulty in this should be obvious: the volume of soil covering the unknown and undetected is so immeasurably vast in comparison with that thus far opened up by excavation, that there cannot be any prospect of ransacking our planet's earthy shell in point-to-point probing with magnetometers and resistance meters or any other instrument of limited range. Until detectors with very much heightened potency can be provided, the outlook for archaeological discovery will not be fundamentally altered by modern science. Neither does it seem very likely that the excavator's time-honored tools of operation—his pick and shovel, trowel and blunted knife—will be superseded in the immediate future.

However he proceeds, with whatever tools he works to discover where treasure lies and to bring it forth from its many niding places, there will be enough to keep the archaeologist occupied for many years to come. There is still treasure aplenty underearth and undersea—even treasure hoards in the popular and romantic sense.

Apart from the ever recurrent search in the waters of Tobermory Bay off the Scottish island of Mull for the gold presumed to lie sunken in the *Florida,* the flagship of the Spanish Armada wrecked by the unseasonable summer gales of 1588, the most recent treasure hunt that has come to my attention is that for the royal wealth lost by King John of England in the estuary of the Lincolnshire Wash. It was there, near Sutton Bridge, in the year 1216 that the king, accompanied by baggage trains loaded with treasure, essayed passage across marshlands that at that time bordered on the sea but have since been filled in by alluvium from nearby streams. In those days the dyked road along the Wash was subject to tidal irruptions too sudden to avoid and too violent to ignore. Overtaken by such a rush of sea, King John barely escaped with his life, while his baggage animals were swept from the causeway and engulfed with all their precious burdens. Today the causeway is no longer discernible, but lies under deep sand some miles inland from the present shoreline of the Wash. In 1957 an English electrical engineer undertook to locate its course by means of resistivity surveying, relying on the difference in electrical resistance between the clay-packed stone roadway and the loose alluvial sand surrounding it. Success attended his efforts insofar as he was able to spot and trace the buried causeway, but at present writing the location of the royal treasure, which must still lie somewhere close beside the causeway, has not been discovered. It is conceivable that a mine detector or a magnetometer will yet find it.

Another and older royal treasure with even greater allure lies underground in Calabria in southern Italy. In A.D. 410, after Visigothic Alaric had taken Rome by assault, he marched southward intending to pass over into Sicily and invade North

Africa. But at Cosenza in Calabria he died of fever. Near there, under the riverbed of the Busento, he was buried with a great accompanying treasure of accumulated booty. It is said that the river was diverted from its course so that the grave might be dug, and the stream afterward led back into its former channel. Those by whose hands the task had been performed were discretely silenced forever, in order that no man might know the exact spot of concealment. It has been suspected that the junction of the Busento and Crati (where there is today a bridge called locally by Alaric's name) may mark the site; but I have not heard that resistivity or magnetic surveys have as yet been put on the spoor of this most carefully concealed consignment. Perhaps some day they will.

RECOVERY AND CONSERVATION

Although there has been here and there a recrudescence of treasure hunting, stimulated by the new devices supplied by science, as if in deliberate reversion to the discredited behavior of former days when archaeological excavation was a promiscuous digging for antiquarian plunder, such in general is not at all the kind of undertaking in which today's archaeologists are engaged, nor the sort of plunder that they seek.

The revolution in excavational procedure that signally distinguishes contemporary digging from the unsystematic and improperly motivated delving for antiquities of earlier expeditions has largely been due to a shift of interest from buried objects to the human history behind them. For this end it was no longer permissible to attend only to those relics of the past that appealed to contemporary taste and current scholarly interests, neglecting as intrinsically unimportant the miscellany of accompanying material evidence. Having no apparent value or unusual distinction, most of this evidence had hitherto been summarily consigned as refuse to the nearest dump. (There are several disconcerting anecdotes about diggers who have redug their predecessors' discard!) But now, abruptly, everything encountered in an excavation was ceremoniously treated with the utmost care and attention; "closed deposits," "sequence of levels," "stratification," "residual context," and other related concepts became the watchwords of the day, dictating a wholly novel code of interests and method to the supervising excavator. Despite their seeming abstruseness, most of these phrases may be construed as exhortations to full and accurate observation and conscientiously exact recording of any and every vestige of material evidence. If they supplied a professional vocabulary for the "science of archaeological excavation," the procedure that they imposed on the digger was pretty much what ordinary common sense might suggest and practical experience might demand. The existence of a "science of excavation" (rather than a practical art of competent digging) is largely illusory. Each dig sets its own problems, which must be solved on the basis of intelligent judgment and a sense for effective improvisation rather than by appeal to an ordered system of rules and regulations.

Beyond dispute, there have been genially gifted excavators endowed with innate talents for their task, just as there have been conspicuously successful excavators on whom favoring fortune has smiled; and there have likewise been diggers and delvers whose excellent projects and sound intellectual equipment and professional training have somehow remained unrewarded by any notable discovery. But whether they have been deft or not so deft at ordering their digs, whether crowned by publicity or left unnoticed by the world, they have kept in mind one cardinal principle: not to ransack the soil of antiquity for fortuitous trophies, but to watch every situation and every development with the utmost assiduity and acuity, neglecting nothing that could in any sense serve for material evidence.

Where this material evidence chances to be in scant supply, as must be the case for investigations into the less abundantly preserved past, excavational methods have perforce been especially heedful and delicate. It is for this reason that those who have investigated prehistoric sites, and who have been confronted with meager and almost obliterated relics from periods as remote as paleolithic and mesolithic man, have become the pioneers in inventing and perfecting skillful techniques for recovering minimal amounts of material proof. Their work has often been a model for others to follow in areas of more generous yield, where there is not always the same compulsion to slow precision. More acutely than their colleagues engaged in nistorically substantiated cultural areas, the prehistorians have realized the responsibility of the excavating archaeologist to gather full and final testimony on the remnant of the past that only too often, by their digging, they irrecoverably destroy.

There could be no better illustration of the profound change in outlook and professional practice attendant on archaeological excavation than the exhumation of the mound of Troy-Hissarlik near the mouth of the Turkish Dardanelles. It was first undertaken in 1870 by Heinrich Schliemann, who had no previous training or experience, continued by him under Wilhelm Doerpfeld's enlightened counsel and direction, still later after Schliemann's death in 1890 prosecuted by Doerpfeld with still more intelligent comprehension of the meaning of stratigraphic levels, and finally after an interval of a third of a century resumed by the University of Cincinnati expedition under Carl Blegen, working on a very different scale of restrained intensity and devoted to the few undisturbed and still significant sectors of the violently dismantled site in order to establish in fuller detail and with greater certainty the chronological sequences and cultural relationships of the trimillennial occupation of the site. A measure of the growing understanding of stratigraphic and ceramic evidence, as archaeological techniques have matured in three generations of diggers, will be found in the altered character of the publications devoted to the results of these recent campaigns. Schliemann, who as first comer to an unexplored site uncovered most of the surviving material—and in so doing discarded the upper occupational levels of Roman and classical Greek times—laid bare the great girdle walls of Troy VI and the foundations of earlier Troy II with its famous gold "treasure of Priam." He summarized these momentous discoveries in three inadequately documented and rather popularly written books on *Troja and Ilios*. Doerpfeld, with far less to add to the catalog of finds, nearly matched his predecessor's literary output in bulk, even as he greatly surpassed him in professional interpretation of the chronological and historical significance of the accumulated evidence. Professor Blegen, in collaboration with a corps of trained assistants, was able to fill an entire series of quarto volumes with little else than potsherds and spindlewhorls and suchlike objects, which had only too frequently been treated as castaways in earlier digging, amid statistics of measured levels and attendant soils, after competently completing the herculean task of gathering, cleaning, sorting, cataloging, and critically evaluating thousands of disconnected material documents to serve as clues to establish (as no predecessor had succeeded in doing) the millennial history of Troy-Hissarlik.

Such an achievement illustrates the paramount necessity for keeping total and meticulously accurate records of all excavational results—records that will seem extravagantly minute by being so undiscriminatingly all-embracing, without distinction of values or apparent interest. All these records must be made on the spot and at the moment of each discovered particle of material, and not written up from recollection afterward or colored by knowledge gained from subsequent discoveries.

The excavator of biblical Gibeon states that "a conservative estimate of the number of pieces of broken pottery which have come from the four seasons of excavation at el-Jib is in excess of 200,000. Each of these sherds has been washed, dried, looked at carefully by at least four pairs of eyes; and the crucial pieces of evidence have been photographed, drawn to scale, and catalogued." (James B. Pritchard, *Gibeon, Where the Sun Stood Still: The Discovery of the Biblical City* [Princeton, 1962].) None of these vase fragments had the slightest artistic merit or any conceivable interest or value except as circumstantial evidence; yet this was sufficient to justify such extravagantly tedious attention.

Very generally and quite unavoidably, excavation destroys the object of its own attention. Where there is vertical strati-

43

fication, as on a continuously occupied area, it is usually impossible to lay bare lower levels without previously removing those above them. Mere removal of an object from its place of discovery is destruction of attendant circumstances and hence obliteration of evidence that might prove significant. The excavator has no title to disregard levels or features from a period in which he is not interested or which seem to him to offer nothing of archaeological moment. He may not, therefore, dissipate or discard or even move from its place of finding the least object without noting the character and composition of the surrounding soil and without measuring, mapping, and photographing whatever is amenable to such attention. Since it is impossible while digging is in progress to foresee the scope or occasion of future professional interest in the matter, there is no means of drawing any division between what may be needed for future study and what may be neglected or discarded as irrelevant.

There are innumerable instances that might be cited as examples of the benefits of fully and accurately kept records. Among these I choose one pertaining to recent American archaeological scholarship. Professor Arthur Frothingham of Princeton, while in Rome in the years 1895-96, was commissioned to acquire Etruscan material for the University Museum of Philadelphia. At that period the Italian government tolerated free-lance excavation and was generous in granting exportation permits for antiquities, with the result that a series of Etruscan tombs at Narce, Vulci, and Pittigliano in territory northwest of Rome were cleared for Frothingham's account, although not under his direct personal supervision. Fortunately he stipulated that plans of all the tombs should be drawn and that exact inventories of their contents be compiled indicating the precise location of each object within its group. The acquired material reached Philadelphia in due course, but it was not until nearly half a century later that a complete and systematic publication of the entire lot was undertaken and brought to completion. In the interval, as may be imagined, memory had lapsed and order had deteriorated; so that a task that might have been accomplished with comparative ease in 1897 now demanded extreme patience in comparing old photographs, reconstituting old notes and memoranda, interpreting systems of numbering and grouping, and reassigning lost labels. But much more than a routine museum obligation was involved. In the days when Etruscan tombs were being plundered wholesale and their contents dispersed far and wide, exact records such as Frothingham insisted upon were precisely what were almost invariably lacking. Yet, once Etruscan archaeology attained maturity and was seriously taken in hand, reliable information on contemporaneous occurrences and local distributions in the various types and forms of Etruscan grave offerings was eagerly sought by professional scholars; without such information they found it impossible to reconstruct the chronological course of Etruscan material history. Although the sparsely surviving writings of the Etruscans can be read, they can be only very partially interpreted; further, Greek and Latin references to this enigmatic race only sketchily report its political, economic, and cultural career. If the previous discussion of "ceramic ladders" and "sequence lists" is called to mind, it will be appreciated that calendar dates and a coherent cultural development for the Etruscan folk can be supplied only by interpolating the correctly ordered Etruscan material into a chronology firmly established for some other contemporary culture—in the present case, primarily that of Greece and secondarily those of Latin Rome and Punic Carthage. It was this wider goal that Dr. Edith Hall Dohan envisaged when she undertook her study of the Frothingham tomb groups. It is a very considerable tribute to the methodological training and conscientious thoroughness of American archaeological scholarship that she acquitted herself of her intricate task with entire success, leaving her monograph on *Italic Tomb-Groups in the University Museum* (U. of Pa., 1942) to be a model of its kind.

Today, happily, such beclouding situations as beset the Etruscologist who attempts to put order into the undocumented miscellanies in the world's museum showcases and storeroom packing cases are no longer apt to recur. The excavator's sense of moral responsibility to succeeding scholars lies too heavily upon him to permit heedless operation; and even the most commercially minded dealer (who necessarily has to establish contact with unprofessional sources of supply) will make every effort in his own interest to elicit concurrent information of time, place, and circumstance for the objects that he hopes to sell.

In the realm of accredited archaeology, where the excavator aims to make a scientific laboratory experience out of digging, he must introduce high standards of precision in observing, recording, and moving the material in which he works, admitting no part to personal bias or subjective error and leaving no opening for casual impressions of the moment or subsequent interpolations from memory. The penalty of thus imposing scientific method is a renunciation of all the pleasurable uncertainties that once attended more promiscuous digging. A competent and very readable account of the punctilious methods and unavoidable monotony of a modern dig will be found in James B. Pritchard's *Gibeon, Where the Sun Stood Still.*

The most recent present-day procedure in excavation involves what may be called three-dimensional recording. A restricted area is divided by stretched wires or other means into a checkerboard of small equal squares. These dividers remain undisturbed while digging moves down into the soil, and its checkerboard pattern is projected vertically by plumb lines to each new level. Meanwhile the checkerboard is transferred at a conveniently reduced scale to the drawing board and reproduced anew for every critically interesting level. In this way the objective content of each distinguishable level or stratum is mapped in correct horizontal geography; and the series of maps, superimposed, restores third-dimensional measurement to the entire complex.

Excellent as such a system of record keeping may be for open areas and certain types of terrain, it cannot be applied indiscriminately to every site. It might even be maintained with considerable show of reason that there cannot be universally applicable rules to govern excavational practice, since every project in one way or another will make its own specific demands upon the excavator's experience, intelligence, ingenuity, and adaptability to current circumstances. It is this that prevents digging from lapsing into standard routine and preserves it as a specialized skill, more akin to the craftsman's extemporizing reaction to his art than the technologist's prescribed precision in repeating preformulated processes.

In any case, whatever method of exploration and uncovery the excavator may employ, he must document his every step and memorialize each current situation and event.

If this manner of retrieving vestiges of antiquity from the soil has become an involved and tedious occupation, the parallel task of recovery from the depths of the sea is an even more toilsome undertaking. Thanks to the present-day insistence that the archaeologist is probing for knowledge rather than digging for plunder, the execution of a fully scientific ritual on the ocean floor at depths of ten to twenty fathoms is an extremely arduous venture. Like photographic reconnaissance from the air, skin diving has been diverted from military uses to archaeological exploration; and deep-sea salvage has taken its place as a recognized branch of archaeological investigation. There is even, centered here in America, an established Council of Underwater Archaeology. At present the advance guard of this council is recruited for Mediterranean waters from a much, older organization, the ancient and honorable company of native sponge divers, who occasionally bring in reports of sunken wrecks they have encountered in the twilight depths where they win their livelihood. The quondam cargoes of ancient derelicts are not easily recovered or subjected to study, since they lie deeply embedded in accretions of marine growth and calcareous sediment. The ships themselves, if they are significantly old, are in general too disintegrated to permit recovery or reconstruction.

In a recent (1960) American underwater campaign, led by George Bass and centered off a rocky headland of southern Turkey approximately halfway between Cyprus and Rhodes, the immediate objective was a wreck of a ship from late Mycenaean times that proved to have been transporting mainly raw copper ingots and tin, the twin mainstays of the late Bronze Age metal economy. No doubt these ingots will throw light on ancient commercial trade routes and other nautical matters; but it is perhaps permissible to guess that, just as diggers on land dig for the love of digging, so skin divers at sea dive for the zest of diving.

It is not too simple and easy a pastime. During the summer of 1960, the skin-diving archaeologists of the Bass exploring party were obliged to descend into eighty feet of water for their daily round of work. At this depth they found that they could remain only half an hour at a time and that it was not advisable to descend more than twice a day. Once safely grounded on the derelict ship, they became only too well aware that submarine excavation is a totally different matter from the pick-and-shovel, knife-and-trowel routine of traditional digging with gangs of workmen and every sort of mechanical facility. Even though one has never wielded a sledge hammer or tapped a chisel under eighty feet of water or tried to measure objects there with a meter stick or to take flashlight photographs in the wet, one can readily imagine how

48

difficult such subaqueous efforts must be. The tools and techniques employed on this campaign were familiar enough—there was even a vacuum cleaner in reverse, in the shape of a long flexible hose hitched to an air compressor up aloft for blowing away loose sediment!—but irksome novel conditions must have made a nightmare of frustration out of the simplest tasks. It is reported that all the objects aboard the wreck were so heavily encrusted with limestone that virtually nothing could be pried loose; but each object, still imprisoned in shapeless lumps of limestone, was hoisted to the surface and there disengaged from its stony envelopment. When the mass was too heavy for hand-over-hand hauling out of the deep, inflated balloons were attached to float it upward to the surface.

All in all, a weighty challenge from inanimate opposition! But skin divers are a dedicated order; and one need not be surprised if these subaqueous excavators, who like Atlas of old "know all the depths of the sea," develop a merman's scorn for *plein-air* grubbing in the dirt. Yet their resort to underwater does not absolve them from the present-day digger's obligation to conduct operations with laboratory precision and to apply (as far as may be mechanically possible) the present-day techniques of scientific excavation.

The excavator's concern for his material discoveries does not terminate with their removal from the soil. A host of practical necessities confronts him as he occupies himself with cleaning, mending, preventing further deterioration, transporting, conserving, restoring, and making available for study and publication his contributions to human cultural history. It must be his endeavor to derive the maximum amount of evidence and information that may be accessible to the mind and eye out of the fragmentary record of the past that time and fortune have permitted him to salvage. Here again, in these extremely practical undertakings, modern physical and chemical science have extended him their aid. To these, rather than to his own

49

experiments of trial and error, are due the recent advances in conserving, rehabilitating, and restoring archaeological materials.

Rehabilitation adds nothing new, but seeks merely to recondition and preserve what has been found. *Restoration* is a different procedure, in that it supplies anew what has been lost, so as to re-create the erstwhile solid shape and appearance by complementing what has survived with what may be confidently surmised to be missing. Where artifacts are concerned, and particularly where these may claim interest as works of art, the normal rehabilitative processes of cleaning, mending, and protecting are frequently supplemented by a judicious modicum of restoration. Especially will this be so when display in museum showcases or public galleries is contemplated. We no longer approve the sanguine enthusiasm of the Renaissance collectors of ancient statuary who insisted on having every headless and even legless or armless antique marble torso converted into a flawless entire figure, at times more intensely classic than Pheidias himself would have carved. The dividing date between this cheerful barbarism and the almost pedantic modern demand for leaving the wreckage of antiquity untouched and unadorned falls in the early decades of the nineteenth century. The pedimental statues from Aegina, on which the great Thorwaldsen laid his healing hands, are fully restored figures; whereas the pedimental statues from the Parthenon, the famous Elgin marbles, have been left exactly as they were found. Yet the natural preference for a total figure in place of its battered remnants has at times reasserted itself almost into our present century. The most redoubtable instance is the statue in Berlin of the legendary huntsman Meleager, the attached label to which used to inform the museum visitor that the accompanying hound had been restored by Professor Wolff from a small fragment of the snout. In defense, it may of course be urged that a small fragment of a snout is a somewhat unedifying museum exhibit. Still, today we show the snout and omit the dog.

There are other classes of objects where the problem of preservation versus restoration takes on a different aspect. Such is the case with ancient coins, those tokens of Greek and Roman numismatic art that have been turned up literally in the hundreds of thousands. Provided that the stamped design and legend are still distinguishable, mere legibility may be of greater moment to the historically minded antiquary than any degree of perfection in the condition and consequent market value of the coin. All three of these desiderata—complete legibility, perfect preservation, and high market value—will attend on coins struck in gold; for gold does not tarnish or corrode even in three thousand years, so that gold coins need no more subtle treatment than washing in clean water. Silver coins, however, may undergo extensive deterioration, either by exposure to air, which causes formation of a black coating of silver sulphide, or by prolonged contact with saline soil, which induces a gray surface layer of silver chloride. Here a little knowledge of chemistry will help undo the damage. In any event it is the excavator's usual experience that unearthed silver coins will permit identification even when they cannot qualify for the collector's tray or the museum showcase. The plight of ancient bronze or copper coinage is much more serious. And bronze is far and away the most common material for coins unearthed by excavation. Having much less intrinsic worth than gold and appreciably less value than silver, bronze coinage was always issued in far greater quantity and also was less carefully guarded by its possessors. The total amount of bronze coins lost, discarded, buried, or otherwise concealed in the soil's hiding places during the course of the centuries is prodigious. Yet it has for the most part survived in poor state; surface conditions of recovered coins range from easily recognizable through conjecturally identifiable to wholly illegible.

Where bronze coins were amassed together, as in leather pouches or metal or wooden boxes, to form what numismatists term a horde, corrosion generally has fused them into a mass of utterly illegible metal. Yet coin hordes are rated as particularly valuable for the variety of information that they may be made to yield.

For cleaning single coins in silver or bronze, warm soapy water and an old brush or wire bristle may be counted on to remove the surface crust; but this treatment has the serious disadvantage of removing and destroying forever the outermost layer of the original design. And the old-time excavator's expectation that a corroded silver coin can be restored to its original condition by inserting it into the heart of a freshly opened lemon hardly ranks as an important chemical precept. In contrast to these primitive practices, the introduction of the electrolytic bath has made available a truly miraculous method of salvage and restitution.

The incrustation characteristic of ancient bronze is the result of oxidation, either from the air or by other contact. Where this formation has been built up progressively without further damage to the surface structure, all of the original metal will still be present, though its outer layer will have been chemically converted from pure metal into that metal's oxide. This straightforward process of conversion can be reversed by reduction of the oxide to pure metal once more and time's deleterious agency can be annulled: the corroded surface resumes its original aspect of smooth clear metal. Actually, such reduction of a metallic oxide is extremely easy to accomplish by attaching the corroded object to the proper terminal of a weak electric circuit passing through a glass tank full of dilute caustic soda or other appropriate medium. An inextricable tangle of illegible bronze coins, seemingly beyond hope for useful study, can be resolved electrolytically into a manageable collection of numismatic specimens. Heavily tarnished and disfigured silver is similarly amenable to restoration by electrolytic reconversion of its incrustation into pure metal.

The procedure is by now abundantly familiar to all museum conservators and should be so to the field archaeologist. In America Professor Colin Fink of Columbia University first called it to the attention of our profession; but I imagine that its applicability to archaeological use may have occurred independently to others in other lands, so that it may be doubted whether it should be claimed as an exclusively American scientific contribution to archaeology. The process can, of course, be applied to metallic objects other than coins. Bronze statuettes, mirror cases, weapons, and armor can all be transformed from ugly corroded masses of metal into the smoothly lustrous and often beautiful objects that they once were.

Photographic illustration of the astonishingly successful outcome of the expert laboratory restoration and reconstruction performed by technicians of the British Museum on the finds from the "Viking" ship-burial of Sutton Hoo and on other archaeological treasures recovered in indifferent condition of preservation will cause the uninitiated to rub their eyes in wonder, so miraculous is the recovery of erstwhile splendor from a seemingly hopelessly tarnished and disfigured ruin. But the miracle is not for every archaeologist unaided by the specialist in restoration. Illustrative material will be found in H. J. Plenderleith's authoritative handbook on *The Conservation of Antiquities and Works of Art* (London: Oxford, 1957). From a consultation of such a treatise it will become apparent that the restoration and preservation of archaeological material is a highly intricate and delicate process demanding first-rate technical knowledge and prolonged practical experience. As such, its more detailed examination hardly falls within the scope of the present survey.

One type of restoration, however, can be performed by wholly unlettered workmen, if they have been trained to the task. It is an operation fascinating to watch, both because of the skill with which it is executed and the satisfactory outcome in which it terminates. I refer to the reconstruction of whole vases from their fragments, particularly when only a minimal number of pieces have survived.

The introduction of the potter's wheel (an event now conjecturally set some five thousand years ago) conferred certain properties on all wheel-thrown vases, which the restorer can turn to profitable account. The process of shaping a vase by "throwing" it on the wheel involves two separate moments of continuous motion—first, that of the turning wheel itself, which produces circular symmetry in a plane horizontal to the axis of revolution; and second, that of the potter's hand, which, as he draws up the spinning mass of clay to give the vase its shape, induces geometric continuity of line in the vertical profile. These two properties of horizontal symmetry and vertical flow serve as guides to the expert vase mender and enable him to reconstitute an entire vase from a relatively small number of unconnected pieces.

Because of the wheel's revolution the potter's fingers leave minute scorings in the form of parallel grooves and ridges on the inner face of the fabric. If an isolated fragment from a wheel-thrown vase is so suspended that these scoring rings lie horizontal, the sherd will be oriented correctly in respect to the vase's vertical axis. And since the horizontal curvature of any sherd is necessarily part of a perfect circle, the full circumference of the vase at that particular level can be constructed. The continuity of flow in the vertical profile facilitates the insertion and adjustment of other sherds at their proper respective levels. Even if the vase showed no surface decoration or pictorial design as a guide to the correct reassemblage of the pieces, the structural information already gained, when combined with some previous familiarity with current shapes and styles, will permit an interpolation in plaster of Paris of all the missing

54

parts of the vase. A correctly shaped and fully formed replica, even of a vase type for which perhaps no complete specimen is extant, may thus be made to emerge from a comparatively scant supply of some of its sherds.

This is not to claim (on the principle of *ex ingue leonem*) that every lone and minute fragment of ancient pottery will permit so spectacular a result. Nevertheless, the paleontologist's well-known feat of constructing an entire prehistoric monster from a few fossilized imprints from its skeleton is scarcely more surprising than the trained vase mender's knack of supplying in plaster, with complete assurance of its correctness, the missing fabric of an almost totally vanished vase. The exploit in either case relies on the correlation of symmetrically disposed organic parts, coupled with a previously acquired knowledge of structure, type, and function.

It will of course be appreciated that there would be no profit in thus restoring all the vases from all the sherds that an excavator may have found in the course of a campaign, however helpful such fully reconstituted specimens might be for exhibition in museum showcases or photographic reproduction in excavational reports. The practiced archaeologist derives more immediate benefit from the unreassembled fragments merely by identifying their type and period and observing the contextual relations of their spot of discovery.

The preceding discussion applies to movable objects of manageable size and appropriate material, such as would normally be lifted from their place of finding and transported to laboratory, study room, or storage.

Quite different considerations come into play where the magnitude of the material is so great and the elements required for restoration are so massive that removal from the field is impracticable. Such is the case for architectural remains and ruins of masonry, whose restoration becomes a matter of rebuilding entire structures or of replacing in position their surviving fallen and scattered or shattered elements. To deal thus with the broken relics of past achievements is indeed to turn back the hands of the clock of time. It is as though one strove to conjure back to life the long dead that once were mighty on earth. But a great fascination attends it. Perhaps it is natural that those who in their thoughts have dwelt so much in the past—the archaeologists, I mean—should feel a compelling desire to see before them in solid shape and material actuality what they have hitherto only pictured to themselves in imagination. Ill-satisfied with understanding with their minds, by aid of measured drawings, photographic views, and small-scale plaster models, the vanished monuments they have unearthed in fragmentary traces, they aspire to re-erect fallen columns, reset crumbled walls, and replace timbered ceilings and roofs, in order to bring back to life a thing long dead. And—professional archaeologists and architectural specialists apart—the general run of educated men and women, whether adept or inexpert in matters antiquarian, derive from well-executed monumental restorations an appreciation and understanding of the art of the past attainable in no other way.

When conceived generously and carried out conscientiously, such enterprises may often prove extremely costly without yielding any commensurate economic return. But if financial hindrance can be removed, there need be nothing chimerical or vaguely fanciful in architectural restoration, even when a structure has been so thoroughly reduced to ruin that little more than token relics of its original appearance remains. Architectural form, by dictation of aesthetic and mechanical law, tends to be repetitive in both plan and detail. This is notably true of Greek architecture and its derivatives in classic tradition; and it is almost equally true of ecclesiastic Gothic and Byzantine building. Indeed, it is apt to be so wherever hewn and fitted stone (rather than undifferentiated brick or amorphous concrete) is the medium of construction. A single well-preserved bay of a

Gothic church or cloister can serve as a model for supplying the other bays that have been destroyed; and an entire Greek architectural order can be accurately recovered from a random sampling of its various structural elements. Almost any ancient Greek temple, provided that its blocks have not all been taken away and its foundations utterly destroyed, could be rebuilt upon its stepped platform with scarcely any deviation from its original state. Where such reconstruction is under debate, the pertinent question is not whether the project is archaeologically sound and technically feasible, but whether it is aesthetically desirable and culturally profitable.

Thus, it would be entirely possible, subject to expert archaeological advice and supervision and a sufficiency of time and money, to rebuild the ancient forum of imperial Rome with a high degree of architectural fidelity and more than a fair share of plausibility. But the resulting chronological incoherences, if nothing that was old were permitted to be destroyed or set aside, would make the project unrewarding and largely meaningless. More pertinent would be objections of another kind. Powerful and valid argument may be made against tampering with historic actualities and obliterating the factual record of man's misdeeds and time's mischances. There is strong sentimental disapproval of any attempt to annul the irreversible action of natural forces and human behavior through the centuries. A cogent instance may be drawn from modern reverence for relics of Greek classical antiquity. Even as we no longer restore broken Greek statues, so we should make no attempt at total restoration of classical buildings.

Until the year 1687 the Parthenon displayed to exterior view no damage or defect other than the loss of a few statues from its pediments and the mutilation of some of its metopes. But since that fateful year of collision between Venetian bomb and Turkish powder store, the temple has stood a gaping roofless shell, its coffered marble and timber ceilings destroyed, most of its marble wallblocks missing, all of its interior columns gone, and nearly half of its exterior colonnade toppled and torn apart. There is no question but that the sadly ruined temple could be rebuilt, correctly and fully except for a few pieces of pedimental statuary. Yet when a beginning of such a restoration was undertaken and the fallen and broken columns of the north flank were re-erected by the Greek Service of Antiquities in 1928 with funds subscribed by a group of American donors, there was considerable adverse criticism, not of the accuracy of the work, but that it should be attempted at all. Subsequently an even more vociferous outcry against the further project of setting weatherproof casts of some of the Elgin marbles in their appropriate places in the pediments proved that there are occasions when archaeology must content itself with exploring and explaining the past without attempting to bring it back physically to the present age.

In connection with the technique of architectural reconstruction it may be noted that the missing portions of the re-erected columns of the Parthenon were not supplied from freshly quarried and hence brilliantly white Pentelic marble but were interpolated in cement tinted to harmonize with the weathered russet and golden brown of the ancient drums. In this way the eye is not offended by the crude splendor of new marble, while the mind is not deceived by the textural and tonal harmony between new and old because the use of concrete leaves unmistakable the modernity of its insertion and therewith attests the recent date of erection of the column.

It is a matter of interest that in the course of the restorations performed in recent years on the Athenian acropolis and affecting the Parthenon, the Erechtheum, and the Propylaea, no serious suggestion has ever been advanced for renewing the brilliant colors that erstwhile made vivid the carved moldings and minor structural detail of their architectural orders. Presumably the reason for this (in itself illogical) refusal to restore color to the marble surfaces of a classical building is to be sought in the instinctive conviction that the violent polychromy of ancient Greek architecture would prove highly offensive to our modern sense for art. Here, as in numerous other instances, the objection to a complete rehabilitation of the ruins of antiquity lodges in the aesthetics of taste, which overrides the admitted capacity of the archaeologist to perform a task repugnant to aesthetic judgment.

Nonetheless, much may be justly advanced in favor of architectural reconstruction. Drawings of restored elevations, perspective views, and small-scale models of reconstructed buildings are highly informative; but they do not convey the emotional response and immediate apprehension that attend on physical reality with its solidity of mass, its more than human size and sense of scale and spatial complexity, its drift of light and shadow over perspectively retreating shapes. These only living architecture imparts.

The routine maintenance and repair of monumental antiquities, which is to say, the preservation of existent architecture from the past in order to shield it from deterioration and collapse, is surely an unobjectionable procedure, provided that it is performed conscientiously and without improvisation or mistaken effort to improve upon the old. But where restoration extends to total re-creation of a destroyed building, of which only enough fragments survive to inform the specialist of its ancient state, the situation is admittedly very different. Yet here too a valid plea may be made that restoration reclaims monuments from virtual extinction and serves to make comprehensible to the modern world something created in other times and expressive of bygone ideals. For only in this way, by direct visual presentation in solid form and tangible reality, can the architecture of the past be brought from the realm of books and learned journals and library portfolios, where only the initiate are aware of its existence. A section of the walls of Babylon, whose enameled tiles were imprinted with dragons, bulls, and lions, was rebuilt at full scale in a lofty-ceilinged room of the Berlin Museum. The effect was one that no colored drawings, no photographic detail, of surviving samples from the wall could ever convey.

A notable example of the re-evocation of an all but vanished monument may be appropriately cited here inasmuch as American financial support and archaeological competence were responsible for it. The recently rebuilt Stoa of Attalos near the heart of modern Athens was originally erected in the middle of the second century before Christ as a gift from the reigning king of Asiatic Pergamon to adorn the civic center, or Agora, of Hellenistic Athens. The resplendent two-storied and doubled-aisled marble-colonnaded portico, nearly four hundred feet in length, was destroyed by barbarian invaders after some four centuries of undisturbed existence. Thereafter its ruins were incorporated by the badly depleted but obstinately persisting city into a girdle of fortification walls, to stand with little further molestation for another thousand years. When the American School of Classical Studies undertook in 1931 the formidable task of excavating the ancient Agora of Athens it obligated itself to the Greek government to construct a museum for housing and displaying the finds from the area. When occasion arose to fulfill this pledge, however, none of several suggestions for such a building on or near the site could gain approval from the Greek authorities, who objected to any building in modern utilitarian style in such a context. The resolution of the impasse was ingenious—and extremely costly: it was agreed that the disintegrated ancient Stoa of Attalos, reduced to little else than its foundations and two brief fragments of wall, should be re-erected *de novo* to its exact original appearance and out of the same original materials—Piraeus limestone for the walls; Pentelic marble for the 138 columns, the façade, and the interior trim; and Attic clay from the ancient beds for the oversize roof-tiles. A descriptive pamphlet on the museum gives the following information:

The Stoa was rebuilt in the years 1953-56 by the American School of Classical Studies. . . . Reconstruction was carried out under the authority of the Department of Restorations in the Greek Ministry of Education. The cost was met by contributions from American donors, half the amount being given by Mr. John D. Rockefeller, Jr. The original design of the building was recovered by the Architect of the School's Excavations, John Travlos. Professor Homer A. Thompson, director of the Agora excavations, had final authority.

With only a minimum of interior rearrangement the rehabilitated Stoa was adapted to museum use for the storage, study, and display of the finds from the Agora—the function that afforded the pretext and ulterior reason for its glittering reemergence into the Grecian sunlight. The Stoa constitutes an outstanding instance of the way in which American archaeologists, supported by American financial aid, may cooperate amicably with foreign governments, to the profit of all concerned. The finely conceived (and as finely constructed, equipped, and endowed) Palestine Museum outside Herod's Gate of Jerusalem is a comparable attestation of American collaborative interest in archaeological antiquities (as of the late Mr. Rockefeller's generosity).

An intriguing form of recovery and restoration is dependent upon inference from what might be called negative evidence. This deduces a positive fact from its absence in the surviving state. When the foundation stones of an ancient building have been removed by later generations seeking to secure trimmed masonry blocks without having to cut and transport them from a quarry, the modern excavator of the site must be alert to notice the different color and composition of the soil filling the cutting within which the blocks were pried from their bed. By opening the trench anew without disturbing the irrelevant adjacent earth, the excavator can (on his drawing board) refill the trench with the blocks that are no longer there and thus regain the plan of the nonexistent structure. Similarly, on the Palatine Hill in Rome quite recently, when an area was cleared to bedrock some sunken circular cavities in the rock were exposed. These were clearly man-made; but for what purpose? The pattern of their arrangement suggested that they were post-holes for rude structures that could only have been round huts of the earliest inhabitants of Rome—*ad urbem conditam,* shall we say? In our own country, in the southwestern states and the Tennessee Valley region, excavators on several occasions by careful observation of the composition of the soil have been able to locate the vanished postholes of destroyed Indian houses and by ingenious deduction from these voids succeeded in constructing entire models of the vanished habitations with their walls and roofs correctly set and carried.

In a far different environment of time and place, the Maya ruins of Guatemala, Chiapas, and Yucatan suffer unceasing depredation from tropical vegetation and rainfall rather than from the hands of men. In nearby Spanish Honduras I recall making my way in the summer of 1916 to the little-visited and at that time untended site of Copan and being amazed at the power of tropical growth not merely for invading and overrunning an excavation of only a few years standing, but for actually destroying its exposed masonry with disruptive roots and tendrils thrust into every joint and crevice. Under such adverse conditions the need is not alone for continual clearing, but for checking the unremitting forces of destruction by consolidating, underpinning, and even rebuilding the damaged structure. There is much to be said for this drastic act of total reconstruction. Take, for example, the case of Tikal in the lowland jungle of the Guatemalan province of Peten.

As recently as 1947, Tikal, "the largest and probably the oldest of all the great Classic Maya cities in Middle America

. . . was a 'lost' city buried in the dense tropical jungles of northern lowland Guatemala . . . when Samuel B. Eckert . . . photographed it from the air. . . . Though silent and deserted it had been known for a hundred years and preliminary surface explorations by archaeologists had been conducted on several occasions. . . . Every visitor has been astonished at the great size of the place, and by the heights of its dozens of masonry temples. Thinking of what ought to be done, they have been appalled both at the size of the buildings and at the enormous task of clearing, excavation, and restoration, necessary before the real significance of Tikal could be made known to the world at large. . . . The area of ceremonial courts and buildings . . . is now estimated at more than six square miles. . . . An airfield constructed by the Guatemala Government at Tikal itself has at last made major work there a practical possibility. . . . The area has been declared a National Park. . . . As soon as permanent water is found, private enterprise will undoubtedly install hotel facilities. It is part of our plan to help tourists learn about the past by seeing some of its greatest products face to face. Tikal is being opened up not only for archaeologists, but for the people of America in general, who support them." (*Tikal,* University [of Pennsylvania] Museum Bulletin, vol. 20, no. 4 [December 1956].)

The ambitious long-term project of the Pennsylvania University Museum, to which, with the cordial support of the Guatemalan authorities, the opportunity of uncovering and rehabilitating Tikal has been entrusted, aims at devoting ten years to the site, completing its excavation and "consolidating the masonry of the New World's tallest and most beautiful temples. After a thousand years these are still magnificent, but each year takes its toll and some of them are in danger of sudden and complete collapse. Much repair work is needed, and soon. . . . We shall be saving the great temples and palaces . . . by recording them on paper. But we want also to save them actually, a task which we owe to the future. . . . If we succeed, Tikal will become a breath-taking experience for countless people, and it will teach them directly that a stone-age technology and a hostile environment did not here prevent development of true civilization." (*Tikal, op. cit.*)

Public imagination responds almost hypnotically to such spectacular sights as Tikal or Peruvian Machu Picchu and Sacsahuaman; but it would not be true to say that the interest of the general public or the archaeological specialist is so captivated by the greater landmarks that the humbler and meaner are allowed to suffer from neglect.

At Cornwall and Hopewell Village in eastern Pennsylvania there existed disused, dilapidated, and rapidly disintegrating foundries for working iron ore by the primitive methods and with the crude equipment of the late Colonial and early Industrial period. Unpretentious ancestors of the great steel mills of today, these widely scattered centers illustrated a manner of life and a stage of industrial development typifying American cultural history in a never-to-be-repeated past. Recently their meager ruins have been converted into national monuments by restoring them to their original state in a landscape setting accessible to all and made intelligible by discreet explanation and instruction. Professional archaeological knowledge and practical experience in reconstruction have supplied the necessary technical guidance and ensured the material correctness of every reconstituted element: the hardwood stacked for charring, the carts and sleds for bringing it in, the great wooden millwheel now once again turning in a sluice to drive clumsy pistons for forcing an air blast to the slow hot fire under the ore heaped in the conical furnace. Even the "iron-master's" dwelling has been put in repair and refurnished as of the period of its pride. Compared with the sumptuous installations of Virginian Williamsburg, Hopewell Furnace is a very minor achievement; but there will be—one assumes—few reconstructions on the

64

scale of Williamsburg; whereas Hopewell and Cornwall typify an opportunity occurring widely through all our states for resurrecting into vivid actuality and making intelligibly appealing our nation's past cultural evolution. If such a reconstruction of the past is not to be a distortion or a travesty, eloquent of misdirected energy and idly squandered funds, restoration and reconstruction must be exact in every material detail. Timbers must be handhewn; planks and boards, where so indicated, must be sawn by hand; beams and rafters must be duly morticed and held with wooden pegs; no prefabricated millwork, no cement or modern mix of mortar, no present day paints and pigments may be used; roof tiles must be shaped to proper size, patterned from ancient materials, and fired to proper texture; and so on, through a long catalog of specifications to conform with traditions and discontinued usages that only the archaeologist can determine. An illustration of how heedfully and how successfully such work can be accomplished may be seen again in eastern Pennsylvania, at Ephrata, in the monastic "cloister" (more properly *Kloster*) of an ascetic German speaking sect founded before the Revolution and enduring into the nineteenth century. The disused and empty buildings, bordering on collapse, have been repaired and reconditioned with most scrupulous attention to material authenticity.

There are indications that the rehabilitation of the Ephrata *Kloster* is in no sense a sporadic or locally restricted phenomenon, but reflects a rapidly maturing concern for re-establishing cultural continuity with a past now threatened with total obliteration in the general metamorphosis of social and material conditions. In western Europe, where so much of historic interest and artistic value has survived from the immediately preceding as well as from more distant centuries, governmental authority has long been exercised toward the preservation and repair of monuments from every period and has utilized expert archaeological counsel and supervision in its official services. In our own country, with its brief career of cultural productivity, archaeological interest has been directed mainly to the truly ancient (but wholly alien) past antedating our annexation of the continent. In the Southwest, architectural consolidation and restoration has been practiced with conspicuous success on the excavated cliff dwellings and villages of extinct American Indian communities, in accord with accepted archaeological traditions for dealing with relics of the distant past. But in the last few decades the perspective has shifted to embrace the much nearer present and include our own cultural relics in the category of archaeological remains.

By admitting the professionally trained archaeologist to companionship with the local antiquary, in the recognition that Colonial and early Industrial and even early twentieth century America has slipped away into an unfamiliar and otherwise unrecoverable past, new openings for careers of profitable employment on a high level of intelligent activity will eventuate. The opportunities thus presented should stimulate archaeological study and training throughout our country by creating a demand for a corps of specialists in the field—to the signal benefit of a profession in which the dearth of adequately salaried positions and emoluments has hitherto been a serious deterrent.

✎§ 4 §✎

INTERPRETATION

Oven-baked clay is a peculiarly indestructible material. Extremely resistant to chemical action, it is one of the most stable of all known substances, "rivalling gold itself in permanence." However much the tooth of time may have gnawed at it, pottery is immune to total destruction. A terracotta drinking cup that has been broken and discarded, only to be rebroken many times more through the ages, still survives in its fragments. As in the familiar ballad of the sorcerer's apprentice who cleaves the water-toting broomstick, the immediate result of division is multiplication. Owing to this disconcerting propensity, prodigious masses of ceramic tableware and kitchenware manufactured in uninterrupted continuity since early neolithic times, even while they have been readily and hence very generally broken, have survived total demolition. In whatever regions man has exercised his skill of shaping and baking pots, the surface of the earth remains littered with the fragments of his handiwork. The uneven shape and comparative lightness of the broken sherds tend to prevent them from settling deeper in the soil, while the erosive force of wind and water conspires to lay them bare on every rounded eminence or sloping hillside once occupied by men. One can still today wander over the lightly ploughed fields and uninhabited hillocks of Greece or the Levant and cull pottery fragments that have lain there virtually undisturbed for more than three thousand years.

Because pottery is well-nigh imperishable and because there is an almost inexhaustible variety of shapes in which clay vessels may be formed and of ways in which they may be decorated, potsherds have proved to be the excavator's most frequent as well as his most serviceable clue to the chronological setting and cultural context of man's neolithic and subsequent history. If we leave out of account the coarse undecorated wares of mere utility, there is probably no example of better grade pottery from any place or period of the world that cannot be distinguished by an experienced eye from all other fabrics wherever or whenever produced. This may seem an astonishing statement; yet I should be hard put to it to cite a single instance of ceramic art showing appreciable heed paid to profile and ornament in which resemblance to the productions of some other time and place amounts to complete duplication, or can lead to confusion between two different cultures or between different epochs of the same culture. And further, so compulsive upon the craftsman are the forces of taste, custom, and technical tradition that the ceramic output of any culturally consistent area and of each successive period within that area will always and necessarily maintain its own recognizable coherence of style. Instead of the disordered variety of the novelty bazaar or curiosity shop, where utter diversity reigns, the ceramic output of any given cultural epoch will invariably possess characteristic resemblances sufficient to set it apart and serve to inform the experienced excavator precisely where it is that his delving into the past has brought him. As Sir Flinders Petrie was among the first to point out, pottery is the excavator's alphabet of discovery. For that reason he must familiarize himself thoroughly with the language that it spells out. The untutored jibe at the archaeologist's obsession with battered and broken bits of clay— "always pots and more pots"—fails to take account of his excellent reason for thus paying them so much attention.

Nowhere has the assistance of ceramic evidence been more effective than in digging the city mounds of Iraq. In this region where human occupation has always been closely associated with the life-giving Mesopotamian rivers, habitations have been clustered on riverine eminences rising prudently above flood levels yet low enough for easy access to river water and the irrigation of adjacent land. Inevitably and unexceptionally during long continued occupation (or intermittent reoccupation) of such a restricted dwelling place, airborne dust and manbrought refuse have combined to raise the level of habitation steadily higher through the years, leaving each rebuilding based on the accumulation of its predecessor. As a result of many centuries of this process of deposition, the Mesopotamian towns have lifted to make the conspicuous and often surprisingly lofty mounds that are called tells in native Arab speech. These steep-sloped artificial hills may rise as much as a hundred feet above the original insignificant eminence on which they are based.

When the excavator sinks an open vertical shaft through such a tell and thereby exposes one after another the superposed levels of occupation, he reascends the stream of time as he penetrates downward through the mound. As he proceeds, the major uncertainty besetting him is difficulty of determining at what varying chronologic speed through what unequally distributed periods of time he is moving. In order to recover the historic succession of human habitation (which on a Mesopotamian tell may extend through more than five thousand years), the excavator must construct from the material that he encounters some sort of chronological scaffolding into which to fit the successive strata. Where these strata yield finds as eloquent of their time of deposition as clay tablets with decipherable writing, or carved reliefs with intelligible design, or metallic objects of familiar type, chronological identification tends to be relatively easy and void of error—provided always that the excavator makes certain that these chronological indices are not extraneous intruders into levels to which they do not properly belong! But even where such guides are lacking, there are always pottery sherds. The great need, accordingly, is to compose a reference list showing the vase shapes and fabrics and decorative ornamentation characteristic of each level, attaching to it a notation of such accompanying dates as may have been derived in any manner from chronologically fixed material or ceramic evidence from elsewhere. Although no absolute calendar will necessarily transpire, at least an orderly chronological sequence in ceramic terms will have been established.

Yet the task is not as simple as it may seem. Much more must be done before a "ceramic ladder" to the past can be built without error or omission.

Not every tell or other inhabited site need have had unbroken and continuous occupation through the centuries. The ceramic sequence derived from any one site may have gaps and missing rungs in the ladder. But persistent investigation of a cultural area, covering a considerable number of stratified locations, may be counted on to bring these omissions to light. Items that were not represented in earlier excavations may be interpolated into their proper place of occurrence in the chronological catalog of ceramic types. In this way a master list may be compiled, exhibiting the complete and entire course of ceramic history for a given cultural area.

Were it not for such a master list, the occurrence and duration of the periods during which a site may have stood empty of human inhabitants might prove extremely difficult to detect, if only because a negative state cannot leave a positive trace. When the great city mound of Nineveh was methodically explored by vertical probing, the uppermost layer of comparatively modern occupation was immediately succeeded by an ancient Assyrian stratum; the intervening centuries had left no visible accumulation. On many a Near Eastern site the excavator has passed, as though through a hole in time's curtain, from known historic levels to some remote period behind recorded history. In Greece, likewise, the classical and preclassical sites of occupation are frequently not identical; the excavator may pass from levels marked by modern coins and broken Turkish pipe bowls or Byzantine ceramics directly into soil studded with sherds from Mycenaean or pre-Mycenaean times amid foundations of prehistoric houses without ever encountering any significant relic of the classic age. But a knowledge of the chronologic context of ceramic types precludes any possible misunderstanding of the excavational evidence.

More disconcerting and potentially much more conducive to misinterpretation is the encounter with inverted strata or otherwise displaced levels. It may be taken as a general norm that whenever an era of greatly increased material wealth and architectural ambition ensues upon one more poorly endowed, there will be stratigraphic intrusion by the later upon the earlier, leading to destruction (and sometimes stratigraphic inversion) of the older layer. Thus, it is usually idle to dig through imperial Roman levels of any pretension and magnitude in order to ascertain previous local conditions. The reason why so little is known archaeologically about Rome's original foundation or about the growth of the city through its formative years under the earlier republic—two topics of the greatest historical interest—is not because repeated conflagration has destroyed the older buildings (charred refuse and disused foundations are still informative of past events), but because the prodigious scale of imperial building operations has obliterated the outlines, removed the foundations, and even disturbed the very subsoil of preceding structures.

A comparable condition attaches in Greece to the site of Corinth, where American excavations have been carried on for almost a century with considerable resources, although with occasionally intermittent energy. Yet years of digging have elicited very little information about the prosperous commercial city of the Cypselid tyrants and the Greek classical period. This is partly due to the thoroughness of the Roman destruction of the city in 146 B.C., but even more to the later rehabilitation of the city as the administrative center of Roman rule over Greece. For reasons of much the same nature, elsewhere in

Greek territory—as in many other Mediterranean regions—the prehistoric sites that best repay excavation are those that remained unoccupied during the Greco-Roman age.

But the mere absence of evidence is seldom as misleading as is its deceptive presence when this takes the form of stratigraphic inversion of the true chronological sequence. Such deceptive evidence was uncovered at a prehistoric Anatolian site excavated under American auspices several decades ago. Later occupants of the *tepe,* or settlement mound, had enlarged the summit area inhabited by their predecessors. In order to do so they had leveled the crown of the hill and spread the soil, and all its discard, over the lower slope. The modern excavators cutting a trench diametrically through the mound from its outermost margin encountered at the bottom of the slope the displaced later material from the disturbed upper levels. The original stratigraphic sequence had been reversed; and only knowledge gained from other sites in the same cultural area, where the ceramic evidence had been preserved in correct chronological order, prevented a serious misinterpretation of archaeological history.

And yet, even where, by matching and crosschecking and interpolating the evidence from all properly controlled excavations in a culturally uniform region, a composite and complete ceramic sequence has been constructed, extending from recent levels all the way down to bedrock or sterile soil below every trace of human industry—what intelligible history can be constructed from such a record? Even the most representative collection of human artifacts in chronologically correct arrangement is an unenlightening chronicle unless accompanied by a measured scale of years to permit some sort of reference to social and political developments. Where the excavator has nothing to show except broken pots, clay and stone spindle-whorls, bone netting needles, obsidian knifeblades, metal or semiprecious trinkets salvaged from crumbled skeletons, the tally of years is virtually impossible to take. His "ceramic ladder" can supply cultural sequences, but their chronology will be purely relative. And he will not know with any assurance of certainty what longer or shorter lapses of time should be assigned to the various stratigraphic layers through which he has been digging.

Confronted with this dilemma and lacking any better mode of reckoning, excavators have occasionally attempted to calculate elapsed time from depth of material deposit, as though an accumulation twice as thick as another should indicate twice as long human occupancy. Were this a dependable criterion, inches and feet of gathered refuse could be converted into years at so many decades to the inch or centuries to the foot, and the excavator, as he proceeded to dig through successive layers, would know at what rate he was moving backward through time and where he might at any moment be in the calendar of the past. Such a scheme for estimating time might seem to resemble the meteorologist's familiar convention for reducing a fall of snow to equivalent inches of rain; but there is this important difference that the latter conversion is approximately reliable, whereas the former is not reliable at all. For no one who takes into account the capricious incidence of destruction by fire, flood, famine, and war, and the innumerable vagaries of human ecology, will pretend that such a formula for extracting chronology from stratification can lay the slightest claim to accuracy. Perhaps it may seem to be better than not hazarding any chronological estimate at all. But after various misdirected efforts demonstrated that such a method of evaluation is so precarious as to be worthless, or worse than worthless because speciously misleading, it has been tacitly abandoned by all workers in the field.

In order to gain a footing and find a path through the historically uncertified course of the past, the excavator must somehow manage to attach fixed calendar terms to the various levels of occupation, whose order of their occurrence he knows but not their duration or their remoteness in time. In the jargon of the profession, he must convert relative into absolute chronology. But in order to do so, he must somehow introduce contact with dated materials. The concurrence of these with the material of the various levels will provide temporal markers, signposts (as it were) to guide his penetration into the past. And because pottery is an almost invariable concomitant to every excavation touching man's presence since his neolithic stage, the maximum desideratum for chronological interpretation in archaeological fieldwork would be a device for determining the absolute physical age of potsherds without reference to their place of finding or any other attendant circumstance.

Perhaps the emergence of such a deus ex machina upon the scene, to rescue the baffled excavator, will be deemed in the highest degree improbable and dismissed as mere wishful fantasy. Yet modern science wields wands more magical than those of fairy tale; and it is not beyond the scope of scientific invention to deal thus with the thousand-year-old specimens of baked clay that the digger unearths.

No one who is aware of archaeology's primary concern with chronology will deny the revolutionary import of a technique that could attach absolute dates to ceramic specimens, so as to convert their scattered testimony into an accurate chronometer for human history. Whether their revelations referred to neolithic or Bronze Age or Iron Age contexts, they would be almost equally welcome and of almost equal assistance to archaeological studies.

There are, to be sure, certain more familiar periods and fields of investigation, in which the introduction of absolute dates from ceramic evidence has already been successfully performed. On the basis of internal indications—i.e., records and monuments—it has very generally been possible to assign calendar dates to ceramic material of historically attested, literate civilizations. A culture so greatly addicted to literate recording, so extensively represented by material monuments, and so exhaustively subjected to scholarly scrutiny as ancient Greece in its classic phase makes possible a remarkably close and accurate time schedule of its ceramic productions. Greek vases manufactured between 650 and 350 B.C. (and in particular those of Attic workmanship) are datable with considerable confidence to the decade during which they were made and marketed. Greek vases therefore are as strictly controlled chronological indices as are Greek coins or most Greek inscriptions.

On the other hand, beyond such intimately documented territory, whenever excavation penetrates illiterate and unchronicled domain and ceramic types lose contact with historic record, the excavator despite punctilious attention to every shred of evidence will be beset with great uncertainty. Thus, while the chronology of Greek painted vases may be claimed to be firmly established for the periods subsequent to the eighth century B.C., that of the preceding geometric phase of decorative design floats in a dusk of doubt. The still earlier "Helladic" output of the Mycenaean and proto-Greek era, unilluminated by chronicle of written history except for occasional apparent contact with Egypt and the Near East, can be classified in archaeological terms but cannot be correlated with any demonstrable calendar of years. Even where knowledge and use of writing existed and its extant specimens are intelligible to modern philological scholarship, as in Mesopotamia during the third millennium before our era, the temporal scaffolding may remain insecure. Excavators in that region identify the stratified levels on their sites as *Uruk* or *Early Dynastic* or *Jemdet Nasr* or *El-Obeid* (which are purely archaeological and not historical terms) without venturing any but the most tentative calendar setting for these phrases. Elsewhere in the multifarious regions into which the archaeologists have of late been probing—on the North and South American continents and in many hitherto unsearched parts of Asia and Africa—wherever no written history tells the tale there is no archaeological understanding of the passage of time in human keeping. Where this is true, a ceramic chronometer running true to astronomic time would resolve the major problem still perforce left unresolved—the problem, I mean, of finding the answer to the layman's simple and entirely reasonable query *"When did all this happen?"*

This, then, is at present writing the archaeologist's great quandary—that he can everywhere unearth the evidence for man's past and track his progress through the centuries; yet only too often he cannot tell where at any given moment he is standing in time's labyrinth. For lack of this knowledge he cannot compile with any conviction of their trustworthiness the host of unwritten chapters in man's cultural history. In order to repair this ignorance, his urgent need is for some manner of objective analysis to tell him the age of the artifacts that he uncovers, in order that by assigning to each its date of making and using, he can convert the relative chronological sequences in his materials into absolute calendar time.

At first sight it would seem to the highest degree unlikely that the archaeologist's need, however urgent, can possibly be satisfied. It is difficult to see how any type of physical or chemical analysis, or similar procedure, could be expected to determine on independent internal evidence the age of a human artifact *as an artifact.* The archaeologist is not concerned with the *material* antiquity of the substance in which the artifact has been formed. The clay of which pots are made; the metals in tools, weapons, ornaments, and coins; the wood in structural timber and household utensils; the bone and ivory shaped to human use—all these have their own material age during which they have existed as mineral or vegetable or animal substance. The archaeologist does not inquire into the chronology of the materials as such; rather, he demands to know the date of their diversion to human service, and the relatively fortuitous event of such diversion does not seem to offer any clue to its detection. The clay of which a vase is made possesses a geologically remote antiquity extending back to the era, perhaps millions of years ago, when it was laid down in the bed from which the potter got it. The temporal moment of the vase's manufacture or of its consignment to burial or other mode of arrival underground has no conceivable connection with the geologic age of the clay. Similarly, the antiquity of a piece of iron or bronze, chemically and physically, can hardly be coincident with the moment of its smelting or casting (although perhaps its superficial incrustation with rust or patina may permit some calculation of the time requisite for forming this accretion). Again— though this is a problem of a somewhat different order—it would appear to be a singularly delicate matter to determine from an excavated specimen of wooden haft or bowl or spoon how long ago the growing tree was felled, or by examining a piece of ivory or bone to decide how many years have elapsed since the death of the animal from which it was taken. And yet the situation proves to be by no means desperate.

The elementary distinction between organic and inorganic matter is an important factor. Organic matter is, of course, a constituent of living things only, whether these be animal or vegetable in kind. Precisely because such things live, they are subject to the chemical changes that ensue on death; and it is this moment of suspension of organic processes that initiates the physical state in which the living substance endures as lifeless matter. But this is also the moment of time that specifically concerns the archaeologist in his quest for chronological data. Organic death attends the conversion of growing timber or vegetation into material for human use; and it is this event that stamps upon them their archaeological date as artifacts—as roofbeams or rafters or shingles in houses, as wicker withes in panniers or creels, as wooden platters or ladles or bowls. Similarly the translation of flax into linen, of animal hair into cloth, of animal bone into needle or pin or ornament, and the transition of breathing man into inert corpse, are all archaeological moments, the occurrence of which should approximately coincide with consignment to the place in which the excavator has encountered them. In contrast, mineral matter whether metal or rock, crystal or gravel, undergoes no comparable chemical reformation on being put to human use or discarded from human service. Since the material of a vase never lived, it is as indifferently dead whether it exist as unmined clay in the pit, as levigated lump on the potter's wheel, as painted jar on shelf or in tomb, or as broken sherds in an excavator's trench. (Or so one would suppose!)

For the reason just advanced—namely, that there is a moment of physical change closely contemporary with the date in which the archaeologist is interested—the prospect for chronologic analysis would seem to be much more favorable for organic rather than inorganic substances. This has not proved to be altogether the case. The recently inaugurated science of "archaeometry"—(to borrow its title from that of an annual bulletin issued by an Oxford research laboratory)—has not found itself obliged to confine itself to organic specimens, although progress has perhaps been more spectacular with these. But since theoretic approach and technical method are entirely different for the two categories, it will be well to keep them separate in any discussion of them. And since organic archaeometry has been longer in operation, is more widely practiced, and has given more conspicuous proof of its power of revelation, it should be given prior place in this essay. And further, because it is of American invention and even now, although given worldwide recognition as an innovation of almost unforeseeable significance to archaeology, is most intensively exploited in

American research centers,[1] it merits particular attention in a survey of American contributions to humanistic studies.

Radiocarbon Analysis

All living organisms ingest and therewith accumulate carbon internally throughout the term of their life. This results from the absorption and assimilation of food and air, on which the organism relies for maintaining its existence. Animals, in taking air into their lungs by breathing, retain some of its component oxygen in their blood, and return the rest to the atmosphere without assimilating the gaseous carbon (dioxide) that it contains. They do, however, in devouring their food, bring carbon compounds into their digestive tracts and retain these in one form or another in their systems. The dietal economy in the vegetal domain of life works on a different system. Vegetable "breathing" consists in converting by catalytic action, with the aid of the chlorophyll in the leaves, the carbon dioxide in the air into hydrocarbons; these are retained as food, while the component oxygen is returned to the atmosphere. Accordingly, carbon is accumulated to a much greater extent in plants, trees, and other vegetal growth than in animals. (It will be familiar to everyone that the fossilized vegetable matter that we call coal is mainly carbon.) It is because of this greater carbon content that radiocarbon analysis has been directed to vegetable relics of the past in preference to animal relics.

The process of ingesting carbon continues through the lifetime of every organism, both animal and vegetable, and the accumulated store of carbon remains in the animal skeleton and in the surviving structural fabric of the tree or plant or vegeta-

[1] There are at present some forty centers for radiocarbon analysis in the world, and more than half of these are located in the United States.

79

ble fiber. An extremely minute fraction of this carbon store will be radioactive—for a reason that cannot fail to seem highly mysterious to the scientifically uninitiate.

The unremitting bombardment of the earth's atmosphere by cosmic rays from outer space occasions the conversion of an inconsiderable (yet in their aggregate not completely negligible) number of fortuitously encountered atoms of nitrogen in the air into nuclei that promptly disintegrate to produce atoms of "heavy carbon." This is a radioactive variant of the common form of the element and is distinguished by chemists with the symbol C^{14}. These newly created radioactive carbon atoms in turn do not long endure intact, but combine with oxygen atoms in the atmosphere to form carbon dioxide. As might be anticipated, this differs from the normal and vastly more plentiful variety of the gas by being radioactive. By virtue of the ceaseless circulation of the earth's atmosphere, the constantly forming molecules of radioactive carbon dioxide are mixed and blended with the enormous mass of ordinary carbon dioxide in the air and thus dissipated far and wide over the earth. The outcome of this extraordinary nuclear performance is the equitable diffusion throughout the terrestrial atmosphere of an excessively minute amount of radioactive carbon.

To speak of carbon 14 as radioactive is to say that its atoms are in a steady state of disintegration by emission of radiating particles. This is, however, an extremely leisurely activity, proceeding at an unvarying rate and neither accelerating nor retarding with lapse of time. Geiger counters and other instruments of detection have been directed at these emitted particles in order to record their frequency and supply data for calculating the rate at which the atomic degeneration of C^{14} progresses. For convenience in making arithmetical computations such a rate is usually expressed in terms of a "half-life period," by which is meant the length of time in which any existent store of radiant energy will become reduced to half its previous amount.

The utility of the half-life formulation may be shown by a simple example. If the frequency count of particles emitted from an organic remnant under test is only an eighth part of what it should have been when radioactive distintegration began at organic death, then it follows (since $\frac{1}{8}$ is $\frac{1}{2}$ of $\frac{1}{2}$ of $\frac{1}{2}$) that three half-life periods must have elapsed since that death. Thrice the number of years that such a period comprises will therefore represent the number of years that have elapsed since the date of decease. It is not necessary to know the *amount* of radioactive carbon originally present in the organic speciment. It is the present stage of disintegration that gives the clue.

One might well be suspicious of such a show of necromantic skill. But if any advantage has been taken of lay credulity and lack of scientific knowledge it should be a simple matter to expose it by a direct test, by giving the practitioner a relic whose date we know on archaeological grounds but of which he is ignorant, and let him tell us by radiocarbon analysis how old he claims it to be!

At the outset we might be inclined to challenge the validity of the estimate of carbon 14's half-life period—and with some show of reason, since the first attempts at evaluation disagreed widely among themselves and agreed only in assigning to it a magnitude of the general order of five or six thousand years. Rather arbitrarily, a weighted average of several discrepant estimates was taken and the half-life period of decay of carbon 14 was set at 5,568 years. Using this figure as a basis, a number of chronometric analyses were performed on organic material submitted by archaeologists, and the reliability of this value enjoyed widespread acceptance. However, the American daily press of January 10, 1961, reported an announcement by the National Bureau of Standards in Washington to the effect that a more accurate evaluation at 5,760 years had been obtained. This revised estimate would increase the antiquity of all previously examined organic relics from the past by three and a half years per estimated century. Retrospectively such a correction is not of great significance, since under previous laboratory procedure there existed a margin of uncertainty considerably in excess of the error in the original evaluation. But with current refinements in technique capable of reducing the uncertainty in carbon 14 archaeometry to as little as one per cent of the estimated time lapse, there is much more pressing need to define the rate of radioactive decay for C^{14} (on which all chronological calculations depend) with the closest possible approach to total accuracy.

It is therefore not surprising that the 1961 pronouncement of the National Bureau of Standards is currently being checked by other research stations, notably one in Stockholm and another at the Argon National Laboratory in Maryland. Since it is not expected that the results will appreciably modify the most recently assigned value, the practice of radiocarbon chronometry can hardly be criticized by challenging its reliance on an inexact assumption.

It is, however, clear that other less easily confirmed assumptions have been made. The half-life period of radioactive carbon can be turned to account for dating organic matter derived from an archaeological context only if the proportion of radioactive to ordinary carbon is a fixed and constant quantity wherever and whenever C^{14} is associated with the common variety C^{12}, both now and in the past. Strictly this cannot be true, since the enormous amounts of coal and other fossilized vegetable fuel that have been burned in the course of the modern industrial era have returned an appreciable amount of carbon to the air without any radioactive content (because the age of these fossil fuels is so great that all their radioactivity must long ago have been dissipated). Correction can no doubt be made for this anomaly; but it is possible that there have been other equally disturbing factors in the past, the extent of which cannot be determined. For one thing, the theory of radiocarbon dating postulates that there is a constant balance, automatically maintained both now and in the past, between the amount of C^{14} coming into being under the impact of cosmic rays and the amount passing out of existence by radioactive decay. It is asserted that such an equilibrium must exist by physical necessity and that it established itself aeons ago when the total quantity of C^{14} present on earth reached sixty metric tons. Even so, this normal equilibrium could be disturbed, for longer or shorter periods, by any one of a number of eventualities.

Thus, it is not certain that the bombardment of the earth by cosmic rays has been uniform through the centuries. In the past it may have fluctuated; in which case our planetary supply of radioactive carbon would have been increased or decreased sporadically. Again, the planetary atmospheric circulation may suffer cyclic changes, leading to uneven distribution of the radioactive carbon atoms; and there may be depletion of C^{14} from the atmosphere during abnormally wet periods and relegation of more of it to ocean depths than is normally recoverable for the atmosphere. Again, there may be alteration in the radiocarbon ratio incident to the physiological processes of ingestion by living organisms. In short, because of factors such as these, the carbon 14 cycle of creation, diffusion, and decay may be—like our planetary climate itself—in a constant state of inconstancy.

For all these disturbing influences there may be remedies. There are other difficulties of a more purely practical kind. Of this latter sort is an inconvenience, which may be troublesome, caused by the laboratories' demand for a rather considerable mass of material for every test. This may not be readily procurable, especially in view of the fact that the sample will be completely destroyed in the course of analysis. There is a further stipulation that the submitted specimen must be from a single and uniform source that has not been diluted with objects of varying antiquity or associated with influences disruptive to its chemical composition such as continual exposure to humidification by ground water. There is no indicated need for precaution against more recent radioactive contamination incurred through the incidents of excavation, removal, packing, and transportation from the original site to the generally remote analytic station, because carbon 14 is insusceptible to radioactive enrichment or impoverishment from contact or exposure. The laboratory technician must, however, be careful to ensure for his workroom a completely neutral radioactive environment, lest intrusive particles affect his counting in the final stage of his tests.

Some of the practical details of laboratory procedure in radiocarbon dating may be of interest. In the original procedure initiated at the University of Chicago by Professor Willard Libby (to whom belongs the entire credit for devising carbon 14 chronometry), the organic carbon was analyzed in its solid state. A more recent technique, at present very generally in use and first employed by de Vries of the Netherlands and Ferguson of New Zealand, reconverts the solid carbon into carbon dioxide. This gas is then subjected to successive stages of purification in order to rid it of any traces of other elements that might add intrusively to the radioactive emission count. Thereafter it passes into a receptacle, surrounding which a battery of Geiger counters picks up and counts the emitted rays. Despite the fantastically slow rate of radioactive decay (which 100,000 years would not entirely consummate), and despite the scarcely imaginable minuteness of the mass of "live" carbon present in the gas, there are enough of the particles emitted every minute from a gram of substance to permit a measured steady count. The walls of the receptacle through which they escape are heavily shielded against the persistent universal bombardment of cosmic rays. Actually, complete protection is virtually unattainable. But the unwelcome intrusion of contemporary cosmic rays can be discounted by making them pass through a separate array of

Geiger counters before they reach the material undergoing test. By subtracting their count from the gross total, their uninvited contribution can be removed from the computation.

All these matters of practical procedure are the immediate concern of the physicist; the archaeologist, however deeply impressed by their ingenuity, is primarily interested in their utility for his own professional ends. With these ends in mind he will be the first to realize the enormous importance of radiocarbon analysis for ordering the cultural past of mankind. In prehistoric archaeology it will introduce revolutionary developments by supplying otherwise unobtainable chronologies. There is an impressive array of archaeological types of material to which relatively exact dates can hereafter be attached by C^{14} analysis, ranging from relics of higher forms of organic life such as human and animal skeletons, artifacts in bone or ivory, hair matting and woolen cloth, to vegetable products such as wooden furniture, architectural timber, charcoal, rope, rush and wicker baskets, cotton and linen—all of which may be present in ancient burials in undisturbed context with other objects of cultural or anthropological interest. For the archaeologist, therefore, the all-important consideration is whether radiocarbon dating is efficient, reliable, and universally applicable within the limits claimed for it. In order to supply an answer to this query, radiocarbon analysis has been put to controlled and critically decisive tests of its reliability by assaying relics of organic material for which there existed an archaeologically or historically established date. There is no lack of such material.

In Egypt, where an almost rainless desert borders the river valley of the Nile and the ancient inhabitants buried their dead in the arid "red land" above the "green land's" flooding, organic material in archaeological context has survived in remarkably perfect condition. Unplundered graves have been discovered for which a narrowly precise date can be deduced from various indications, especially when hieroglyphic inscriptions are present. Thus, to cite an illustrious example, Tutankhamen's entombment may be set on historical evidence within a year or two of 1350 B.C. The decorative designs and hieroglyphic inlay of his grave furnishings make it certain that these were manufactured either immediately after or only shortly before his death. Although the historical importance and the worldwide celebrity of this particular treasure make it unavailable for the destructive process of carbon analysis, less intrinsically valuable organic remnants of equally well-determined date and of the same or even earlier period have been secured from other Egyptian tombs. When these were subjected to radiocarbon analysis in the laboratory of the University of Pennsylvania, the given "known" dates and the acquired "C^{14} dates" were in approximate (although not in exact) agreement.

In one instance, where archaeology assigned a date of 1303-1290 B.C. to a wooden beam because it bore a cartouche of the pharaoh Seti I, analysis pronounced the beam to be from a tree felled more than a century (possibly as much as 225 years) after his death. In another instance a sample of cedar wood from the sarcophagus of an Egyptian noble who, according to Egyptological calculation, lived in the twentieth century B.C. was pronounced on analysis to be from a tree felled in the eighteenth century B.C. When organic specimens from Egypt's Ancient Kingdom were analyzed, even more serious discrepancies between ancient history and modern science eventuated. The new evaluation of C^{14} half-life period will push the carbon dates back about 120 and 140 years for these two instances, but even so will not wholly reconcile C^{14} analysis with chronicled history.

Under very different conditions of time and place, in Peru, bygone cultural phases that must have been spread over many millennia have been classified and put in temporal sequence by present-day archaeologists, both native and foreign, who have greatly intensified the study of the ancient American civilizations. When their labors failed to produce even approximate

86

agreement on chronology in their count of calendar years for the various phases, recourse was had to radiocarbon analysis as to a higher court of appeal. Several pertinent specimens were submitted to laboratory test. The resultant verdict might be expected to have been accepted as final. But this was not the case. On the contrary, those who did not find the radiocarbon dates compatible with their own chronological views summarily rejected them as invalid.

Their action should not be interpreted as an outright dismissal of the entire principle of radiocarbon chronometry or as an indication of any reluctance to admitting its findings in an archaeological court of inquiry. In this particular case, it was claimed that the submitted samples were too few in number, that they had not been collected with proper safeguards against intrusion by chronologically unrelated matter or other sources of contamination, and that these and other similar factors have vitiated the results of the tests. Admittedly, all these objections could be overcome if new and more abundant organic material were collected under more accurate controls. The prospect for a final agreement on Andean chronology through radiocarbon dating is by no means unpropitious.

It is of course arguable that the reported discrepancies attaching to very old material, such as that from early dynastic Egypt, should be ascribed to error in our archaeologically constructed timetable for the civilization from which they derive. But in several instances it is more probable that the radiocarbon dates are faulty. If so, this is not because laboratory techniques are unreliable, but because improper assumptions have somewhere been made in the theoretic frame within which the method has been built.

In this connection a series of tests, which may prove to be the most significant yet performed, was carried out during the summer of 1961 in the radiocarbon laboratory of the University of Pennsylvania in Philadelphia. Various items for analysis were secured from a single and hitherto wholly undisturbed source, the great burial mound at Gordion in Turkey familiarly (and in my opinion correctly) referred to as the Tomb of King Midas, a semilegendary but at the same time strictly historical person who met his death about the year 700 B.C. The following items were submitted to radiocarbon analysis: wood from a log of the outer wall of the tomb chamber, wood from the inner wall of the chamber, wood from a three-legged table beside the king's couch, food (?) from a bowl once set on this table, and shreds from a woolen coverlet spread over the corpse. Presumably these various material items were of closely contemporary origin. Yet radiocarbon analysis asserted that they were not. According to the critical central dates determined for each, the table was made in 715 B.C., the food in the bowl was prepared in 752 B.C., the coverlet was woven in 778 B.C., the log from the outer tomb chamber wall was felled in 851 B.C., and the log from the inner chamber wall was hewn in the year 1099 B.C.

However, the situation is not quite what it seems.

Radiocarbon analysis does not pretend to reveal absolute calendar dates, but admits a possible leeway of at least half a century and in certain cases as much as two hundred years on either side of the central critical finding. By taking advantage of this margin of uncertainty it would be possible to maneuver the table, food, and coverlet into the same decade, and this decade could be chosen to agree with the pre-established archaeological-historical date at the close of the eighth century B.C. But this would be tantamount to conceding that a completely accurate date can be determined by C^{14} analysis only when the historical date is already known to the analyst! The wooden logs from the enclosing walls of the tomb, however, cannot be placed in the same decade as the table, food, and coverlet; one of the logs, in fact, maintains nearly three hundred years' priority to the other objects. A peculiar circumstance may here save face for C^{14}

analysis and restore it to the road of righteousness from which it seems to have strayed.

It is familiar knowledge that growing trees normally add a new ring each year to their trunk's circumference. Each of these rings will of course contain its quota of radioactive carbon; but it is rather remarkable that the successive rings are sufficiently distinct to prevent fusion or mutual exchange of content or subsequent addition of material. Each ring lives its life apart. But this means that in each ring the long process of radioactive decay has begun from a different date—the date when the ring was formed on the tree. There is therefore no such thing as a carbon date for a tree. There is the date of its outermost ring when the tree ceased growing; there is the date of its innermost core when arboreal life began; and in between these two terminal dates there are all the intermediate dates of the years through which the tree was alive. Radiocarbon analysis, consequently, cannot assign a single date for a tree, but reveals the dates of whatever rings from the tree have been submitted for analysis. The logs for the Tomb of King Midas had been hewn from trees of great age and had been squared into beams by cutting away their outermost growth of rings. Hence, perhaps, the discrepancies previously cited.

Herein there is a hint or clue for a possible way of sidestepping the intrusive factors that at present threaten the reliability of C^{14} analysis.

As is well known, our West Coast sequoias may live for two thousand years and more; and if they still stand or if the year of their destruction is known, the count of their rings inward from the outermost is the count of the precise calendar years during which they have been growing and accumulating carbon. Ideally at least, repeated analysis of appropriate samples from sequoias or Douglas firs or piñons can supply the radiocarbon laboratories with the material requisite for constructing a master schedule by which to correct all irregularities and deviations from the simple half-life norm. The project may be laborious and time consuming; but a start has already been made, and each passing year helps to fill in the gaps in the great chronometric inventory by which the future behavior of archaeological studies will be largely determined.

Some such study of the fluctuant "C^{14} calendar" appears to be demanded because it has already been pretty reliably indicated that the deviation between radiocarbon dating and presumed historic actuality (insofar as this has resulted in controlled tests) does not vary directly with the degree of antiquity of the object under examination. On the contrary, it seems to fluctuate rather erratically; it is much less pronounced for certain epochs such as the early Middle Ages of our era (c. A.D. 600-900) and again for the early Greek classical period (c. 700-500 B.C.). As the character of the materials tested can hardly be responsible, some other disturbing factor must be involved, such as fluctuation in the planetary supply (or "reservoir") of radiocarbon, for which correction can hardly be made on a priori theoretic grounds but only on some sort of a posteriori empirical observation using historically dated material to adjust C^{14} deviations. For, whatever incalculable influences may have disturbed the norm in the past, their combined result must inevitably be recorded in the materials themselves. If a sufficient number of specimens with preassured dates from consecutive periods of time can be subjected to radiocarbon analysis, the corrections necessary to reconcile present estimates with historic fact can be elicited and a graph or formula established for interpolating these deviating values into the standard norm. In this way a chronological schedule for C^{14} analysis could be constructed on the basis of material documents of known antiquity. With this in hand, application of the schedule could be made to other material of unknown age within the limits of the established timetable.

Until such a schedule has been constructed, and so long as radiocarbon analysis admits as unavoidable a considerable range of methodological uncertainty in its findings, what value should be attached to the much publicized miracle tool of C^{14} dating? The following estimate is offered purely as a personal opinion.

Under present procedure, and presumably for some time to come, C^{14} analysis cannot pretend to supplant, or compete with, accepted archaeological methods for dating material for which archaeology is in a position to supply historically defensible dates. But where archaeologically derived chronologies are vague, indeterminate, and nebulous—as is the case for most nonhistoric areas and especially for cultures that never reached a literate level—radiocarbon dating is a veritable godsend. Two recent instances will illustrate the far-reaching effect that it has already exerted in prehistoric study.

In a recent review Professor Stuart Piggott remarked that "new radio-carbon dates . . . have forced us to reconsider our schemes of absolute chronology for the Western European Neolithic cultures, and it appears that we were all working on too short a scale. . . . We need many more radio-carbon dates before we can make detailed revisions, but the general trend seems clear."

Even more revealing of the potentialities of C^{14} analysis is the light that it has shed on the unidentified prehistoric people of North America, whose presence in most of our west central states had been deduced from the delicately fashioned quartzite dart heads called folsom points (for lack of a more appropriate name than that of the little town in New Mexico where the first of them came to attention). That the makers of folsom points lived and hunted in a remotely distant past had been proven by the discovery of bones from an extinct species of bison in company with these weapon heads; but the epoch to which bison and hunter belonged remained otherwise completely obscure until radiocarbon analysis pronounced them contemporary with the last of the paleolithic cave dwellers of western Europe at the termination of the last great Ice Age.

What more the future will bring must await the future to reveal; but it is already apparent that radiocarbon analysis is destined to revolutionize entire areas of archaeological investigation.

Inorganic Archaeometry

It must be taken strictly into account that the tests of radiocarbon analysis are not applicable to other than organic material. Inorganic substances undergo no fundamental change on being diverted to human use. Having never lived, dead matter remains dead on being converted into tool, weapon, ornament, or work of art; it experiences no vital impact comparable to that which starts the radioactive clock when a living organism dies. Accordingly, radioactive analysis can force neither earthenware nor metalwork to reveal the date of its manufacture. If any alternative technological device to effect this end could be contrived by science, it would be greeted with enthusiastic welcome by the archaeologists, who are by now aware that their chief function, in addition to gathering and preserving material specimens of man's past cultural achievements, is supplying the chronological setting to man's civilized evolution.

At present writing, the prospect for such accessory devices to radiocarbon analysis, to be effective for inorganic substances, is by no means discouraging. Inorganic matter is susceptible to various kinds of chemical change. It is conceivable that the onset of certain such changes will coincide with the adaptation of metal, stone, or clay to human service. The difficulty lies not so much in identifying the chemical process as in measuring its duration. Thus, the exposed surface of all metallic objects (except those of pure gold) is chemically altered by contact with air, water, or soil. If this action has been continuous, the resultant product is a consistently cumulative accretion. Its physical amount is precisely measurable. But to estimate the time that has elapsed for its formation is a much more difficult matter, because the rate of action is highly variable and may be wholly erratic. An iron knife or spearhead may rust into complete disintegration in a few decades or, under more favorable conditions, may survive intact for centuries. The surface condition of an ancient coin will not, of itself, disclose its antiquity. Bronze objects develop a characteristic surface discoloration in chromatic tones that may entrance the collector, who appreciatively views patina where the less aesthetically susceptible chemist discerns only a superficial deposit of copper carbonates. Since it is an accepted and instantly recognizable indication of antiquity, patination is included by the modern forger among his imitations of authenticity; and it is true that between the gradually formed patina that age imparts and its rapidly created counterpart that the forger produces by chemical bath or applied lacquer there is a difference in physical constitution that the expert technician can detect. It does not appear to be possible, however, to elicit the precise age of genuine patina by microscopic, spectroscopic, or any other available method of examination.

The term *patina* may also be applied to the surface state of ancient marble, though the chemical processes are of a different order. Marble is crystallized limestone and like other limestone is seldom pure calcium carbonate. Pentelic marble contains a trace of iron; and this, when exposed, oxidizes or rusts sufficiently to impart to the surface a golden brown or russet bloom. Marble is also subject to slight superficial leaching by moisture, whether from the air to which it stands exposed or from the soil in which it lies buried. As in bronze, its surface condition is an indication of its age from the time when human use disturbed its geologic state; but again, the extent of this aging cannot be directly measured or computed. Certain very rough estimates may perhaps be made. Like the artificial patina on bronze, the activity of the forger may be detected on marble. A broken statue of scant commercial value in today's market, the work of some mediocre Roman copyist degrading an older tradition, has more than once been skillfully recut by modern hands to pass as a valuable original in earlier classic or archaic Greek style. Since the block of marble is ancient, through and through, no X-ray or other inspection of its interior structure will reveal any discrepancy of date. But, since its surface has been newly attacked and altered, all attempts at concealing the unweathered freshness of the recently exposed interior by chemical tempering and mechanical tampering cannot deceive the experienced laboratory technician. A gross distinction between ancient and modern production can thus be drawn (let us hope to the continued discomfiture of that most unwelcome intruder upon archaeological studies, the unscrupulous forger!); but the fine determination *temporis acti,* which would confer upon metalwork and carved stone as exact a dating as carbon analysis brings to organic matter, still awaits some clever scientist's inventive inspiration.

Fortunately for the excavator intent on discovering dates for his archaeological data, there usually are other substances in addition to stone and metal among the inorganic material that he unearths; and for some of these there is better promise of an effective technique of chronological analysis. Chief among these substances—although, unfortunately, far from prevalent in most excavations—is glass. This is an artificial product whose manufacture, now universal, harks back in central Europe to Roman times and on the eastern borders of the Mediterranean to a considerably more ancient period. Next to glass and second to it in rank as "archaeometric" material (despite its occurrence in virtually every excavation) is terracotta, or baked clay, the material fabric of all pottery and earthenware.

I shall deal first with glass, since the recent discovery of the chronological record concealed in its weathered surface is a novel story quickly told. The credit for originating a method of chronological analysis for weathered glass belongs to an American commercial firm, the Corning Glass Works of Corning, New York, in whose research department Dr. Robert H. Brill and Mr. Harrison P. Hood are responsible for its development. It is therefore, like radiocarbon analysis, an American contribution to archaeological science.

The exquisite iridescence of ancient Roman glass, so highly prized by the amateur collector, is a fortuitous accretion caused by exposure to damp. In its original state the iridescent glass vessel had no such rainbow hues to beautify it, but was of sober, slightly opaque, uniform color. Like the patina that enriches bronze, the iridescence of glass is time's adornment; and like patina, it is a superficial crust. But it is not a deposit of extraneous substance, nor does it involve any reaction to chemical agents in atmosphere or earth. Iridescence is a purely mechanical transformation of the exposed surface, due to a microscopically minute leaching of soluble ingredients in the fabric.

Collectors of iridescent glass often have the disconcerting experience of losing the loveliest patches of color at a touch of their fingers or a sudden draught of air, so fragile are the rainbow flakes. Yet one of these flakes, when removed and subjected to laboratory examination, will reveal a very astonishing property associated with its iridescence and visible under adequate magnification. Although it is seldom thicker than a sheet of paper, the weathering crust from a specimen of ancient glass is made up of a great many hundreds of layers sufficiently distinct to be counted under the microscope. And—incredible as it may seem—the count of these layers will be the count of the number of years during which the glass has been exposed to moisture!

The explanation is as simple as the phenomenon is astounding. Apparently all that is necessary for annual weathering layers to form upon glass is a regularly repeated seasonal variation in moisture and temperature, such as takes place everywhere in the earth's temperate zones. The annually recurrent cycle of atmospheric change leaves its mark in a succession of tiny layers of alternating solution and resolidification, proceeding inward into the fabric. One is reminded of the rings that form, year after year, in outward accumulation around the trunk of a growing tree. Just as the age of a tree can be determined by counting its rings, so the "inhumation age" of a piece of glass can be discovered by counting its crustation layers.

The laboratory tests performed upon select samples of old glass, for which the dates of submergence in water or of exposure to annually recurrent moisture have been established on other evidence, have yielded a concordance in years that would be startling were it not that a simple physical cause makes this agreement inevitable.

The weathering layers of glass may also be compared to the "varves" in the soil, from which geologists derive a count of years extending back to the remote time when the glaciers of the last Ice Age began their northward retreat on the European continent. In fact, the two phenomena are essentially of the same order. Many thousand years ago (about twelve, to be exact) when the great ice cap was melting back over northern Europe, annual thawing and freezing left its mark at the glaciers' icefree edge as a wavelike deposit of alluvial soil. Merely by counting these soil waves (or varves) the geologist can derive the tally of the years during which the process of glacial melting persisted. Counting varves is perhaps not to be classed as an archaeological technique, since it bears only rather indirectly on human material history, but it is a striking example of the similarities in technical procedure that ally present-day archaeology to the physical sciences.

I have compared the annual layers that form on glass through

96

weathering to the annual rings of growing trees. The exact record in terms of calendar years, preserved by tree rings, has been ingeniously applied to archaeology by American excavators at work in our southwest states.

If a cross section of a well-preserved log of unsquared timber from an ancient dwelling is examined, the number of its rings will, of course, correspond precisely to the age of the tree at the time when it was felled. But this information throws no light whatever on the age of the structure in which the timber was set. A certain log from an American Indian dwelling was cut (let us suppose) in the eighty-seventh year of growth of a tree. In what year in the past was the dwelling erected? Obviously, there is no immediate answer to such a question. Yet the technical procedure of "dendrochronology" aspires to supply this missing answer under certain rather closely restricted conditions.

"Absolute" dating in terms of the astronomic calendar of years can be performed by counting tree rings only where the following special conditions prevail: The local climate must be favorable to the preservation of wood; and the species of tree from which structural timber was cut in the past must still flourish in the same geographic area. Whatever the species, it should be an appreciably long-lived variety. Finally, there must have been continuous use of this type of tree with no interruption of sufficient extent to break the dendrochronological sequence.

This last remark requires elucidation.

The crucial factor on which dendrochronology relies is the varying width of the rings in every growing tree. As one year follows on another, its seasons' variable supply of moisture, sunshine, and warmth leaves its record of prosperity or adversity in the year's added growth of trunk. These factors determine the width of the annual rings; and their lack of uniformity down the years creates patterns in the series of rings, sufficiently pronounced and distinctive to set them apart from their fellows. It is presumed that the same growth patterns will be duplicated in the rings of the other trees of the species flourishing during the same period and exposed to the same sequence of climatic influences. If this is so, then the cross sections of trees belonging to different generations (provided that their lifetimes overlap) should present identical patterns amid their rings.

Where the testimony of a still living tree is sought, its ring patterns can be recorded by drilling out a core transversely through the trunk. Since the calendar date of each ring's formation can be derived from its relative position in the series, by mere mechanical count any pattern that the rings reveal can be given the calendar date of its formation.

The next step is to recover a felled specimen of the same species from the same environment in an architectural or similar context of human utility. If this no longer living timber displays anywhere among its rings a recognizable sequence pattern previously encountered in a living tree, the identity of pattern permits the transference of dates to the dead tree (and therewith also to the architectural relic in which it was embedded). Again by overlap, the series of dated sequence patterns can be carried further back into the past, if the dead tree is of older growth than the living one with which it has been collated. If fortune favors the archaeologist by giving him access to still older specimens of timber, he will be able to construct a chronological ladder of firmly dated ring patterns. If the species of trees on which the ladder relies is unusually long-lived, the dendrochronologic advance into the past may be reckoned in many decades at each successive step. Species such as the West Coast Douglas fir and piñon answer to this description; and it is common knowledge that many of the western sequoias are still alive and vigorous even though they began to grow long before the birth of Christ; from all of which it may rightly be concluded that the potential range of dendrochronological determinations is truly archaeological. The degree of precision of dendrochronological dating is comparable to that obtainable from examination of the weathering layers of glass.

Unfortunately, certain inherent difficulties in this ingenious technical procedure tend to diminish its usefulness. Many of these difficulties will occur to everyone who is at all familiar with horticulture; others will promptly disclose themselves when practical application of the technique is attempted. Tree-ring patterns are not so markedly different that it is easy to sort them out or recognize their recurrence in trees of different age, especially as growth need not be exactly the same in different trees but must be subject to each tree's opportunities and experiences. A ring pattern formed during the later years of a tree's life cannot be expected to correspond exactly to the pattern formed during the same series of years in a much younger specimen of the same species. Purely local differences in soil, exposure to light, accessibility to underground moisture, the competition of surrounding vegetation, fortuitous accidents of storm and wind, all play their part in differentiating one individual from another, even when both are geographically and climatically near neighbors. Apparently, only in marginal forest zones close to arid tracts is the fluctuation between rain and drouth sufficiently pronounced to leave a "signature" in the tree rings. Where this condition prevails, the rings are said to be "sensitive," while their congeners from areas of more equitable rainfall are rejected as "complacent." Dendrochronological analysis would therefore seem to be applicable only in certain climatically restricted areas.

Even the seemingly most certain corollary to dendro-analysis, the expectation that past climatic conditions will be revealed by the distribution of abundant versus meager growth in the rings, is falsified by observation of living specimens. The natural supposition that annual tree growth must vary directly with the amount of rain precipitated in the year proves to be fallacious.

So subtle and so successful are the powers of accommodation to adverse conditions in nature, and so complex are the nutritional factors for growth, that tree-ring patterns cannot be decoded into a climatic record. (A specialist in tree-ring chronology wrote: "The ten years preceding 1906 had been severe drouth years, destroying much farm area and causing crops to fail" at Oraibi; yet an enlarged photograph of tree rings from the same general region, published by the same writer, shows no diminution in growth for that particular decade.)

Despite the undeniable obstacles that beset the realistic implementation of tree-ring analysis, dendrochronology has had notable application in the American Southwest, where thanks to a climate favorable to the preservation of wood and the existence of long-lived species of timber trees (notably the piñon) absolute datings of truly remarkable antiquity have been propounded. In the opinion of one authority, "It can be said with confidence that enough *living* trees have now been measured for us to depend upon the sequence back to 1300 A.D."; and correlation with dead timber has carried the chronological ladder more than half a millennium further into the past. Nonetheless, even though practical techniques have been greatly improved for precision and many of the subjective factors eliminated, the professional standing of tree-ring chronology is none too stable. Many of the results have been challenged on the score that the absolute dates drawn from tree-ring data are at times in open conflict with chronologies attained through traditional archaeological procedure.

In strict logic, the foregoing discussion should have been incorporated with earlier paragraphs that dealt with chronological analysis of *organic* archaeological material. It has been introduced at this point because of the striking similarity between the formation of annual rings in trees and annual layers in weathered glass, for each of which phenomena the mere enumerative count of a visible accumulation is used to discover an object's archaeological age. But to revert to *inorganic* substance, it remains to deal with recent attempts to devise effective methods of laboratory analysis for pottery. It is perhaps superfluous to preface their discussion with the remark that such methods, if proved valid and shown to be practicable, would constitute as important a technique of research as radiocarbon chronometry and would inaugurate another epochal period in the application of technological science to humanistic studies.

Attention has already been drawn to a peculiar phenomenon that takes place when clay is baked in a potter's oven. The temperature to which it is subjected is sufficiently high to disrupt the remanent magnetism of the minute particles of iron contained in it. These particles remain demagnetized until the kiln temperature drops again. At a critical point in the neighborhood of 500-600° centigrade remagnetization sets in. This means that all the iron particles will orient themselves to conform to the prevailing magnetic field in which the kiln stands, much as though they were tiny compass needles all swinging to the same magnetic pole. After cooling is complete, and unless reheating to the critical high temperature occurs, the magnetic orientation of the metallic particles within the clay will remain constant, as though frozen in place. An appropriate laboratory technique can determine the orientation and intensity (which is extremely minute) of the magnetized particles in almost any specimen of baked clay such as a potsherd, a terracotta figurine, or a kiln-baked building brick; but the resultant information will be of no archaeological value unless certain other conditions are satisfied.

As every navigator of the seas is aware, the earth's magnetic field is in continuous flux, so that compass readings are at all times subject to appropriate correction if their north-south is to be correlated to the seaman's standard chart. Both the horizontal direction toward which the needle swings and the "dip" at which it tilts up or down are subject to change; but these variations in declination and inclination are not wholly random. Rather, they tend to show a slowly built-up pattern that, to judge from continuous observations extending from A.D. 1580 to the present time, may be cyclical with a career of some five or six hundred years. (This has been denied by other investigators, who claim that the cycle is of very much longer duration.) The remanent magnetization in a specimen of baked clay necessarily reflects the prevailing disposition of the planetary magnetic field at the time and for the place of its manufacture. It must therefore agree with some corresponding moment in a fixed chronological pattern, which is to say, it will reveal the date of its original baking.

For the archaeologist, the chronological bearing of these remarks hinges on the collateral proposition that if

(1) the behavior pattern of the earth's magnetic field can be established for the epoch and the geographic area from which his material is derived; and if

(2) the magnetic orientation at time of manufacture of the given clay specimen can be elicited by analysis of its remanent magnetization; then

(3) interpolation of this second datum into the chronological frame of the first item will reveal the date of the specimen's emergence from the kiln.

So much for a spectacular theory! But what of its more sober practical application?

From the outset it must be admitted that the prospect for "archaeomagnetic analysis" is not very encouraging except for cases in which the specimen for examination has remained fixed in the exact position in which it was originally subjected to effective high temperature. Obviously, such a provision will exclude most of the baked clay objects unearthed in excavation, since these must have been removed from the kilns in which they were fired, with the result that the compass orientation at which they underwent magnetization is unrecoverable. However, there are certain rather unusual situations in which terracotta escapes this ban. Kilns are themselves clay structures and are subjected to the same high temperatures as their contents. Where by chance an ancient kiln has survived total destruction, its walls are a feasible subject for magnetic analysis. Any date thus established will refer to the last occasion on which the kiln was operated (provided that subsequent lightning strike or local conflagration has not vitiated the evidence). Clay hearths in dwellings, clay lined burning pits and brick fire altars are also possible candidates for magnetic analysis, as are mud-brick walls and adobe structures that have at some time been subjected to sufficiently intense heat—a contingency that might attend on sack and pillage of a settlement by hostile forces. But unless, as in such instances, the clay has remained *in situ* undisturbed since its baking, reorienting it in the laboratory in order to ascertain the magnetic deviation of its particles from the present prevalent declination and inclination of the compass needle would be like attempting to measure the length of an object without knowing where to set either end of the tape.

Granted that archaeomagnetic analysis is technically performable on certain restricted classes of clay material, a formidable number of preliminary analyses must be completed in order to compile a master scheme recording the state of the earth's magnetic field throughout the archaeologically pertinent past. Without such a schematic table, an object of unknown date could not be placed in chronological position. There must therefore be access to a sufficient store of analyzable material to which appropriate dates can be supplied by archaeologists on their own criteria. Presumably no such cohesive sequence exists. In consequence, only a fragmentary master scheme can be constructed, incontinuous in time and locally restricted in place.

In a report on their archaeomagnetic studies of archaeological material accessible to them in Britain (*Antiquity,* XXXII, pp. 167-78), Mr. R. M. Cook, Reader in Classical Archaeology in the University of Cambridge, and Mr. J. C. Belshé, of the Department of Geodesy and Geophysics of the same university, have defined the program of their collaboration in the following terms:

> Our aims have been twofold. First, we proposed to take samples of fired clay or stone which acquired their remanent magnetization at dates which were known from historical records or archaeological contexts: in this way we hoped to construct for geophysicists a curve of recent variations of the direction of the earth's magnetic field. Secondly, if such a curve could be constructed, we intended to date by their remanent magnetization samples which archaeologists and historians could not date by contexts or written records. Archaeological remains that possess a datable remanent magnetism include pots of fired clay, kilns, hearths, and other structures of clay or stone that have been fired whether by accident or design.

The following paragraphs are reprinted from the same "Preliminary Report" by these two collaborating scholars:

> Attempts to use archaeological remains have, of course, been made several times in the last sixty years, but before Thellier's work none was successful. The reason is that the earlier investigators restricted themselves to pots. They conceded that they could not immediately determine from a pot what was its angle of declination (or compass-bearing) at the time when it was fired. But they assumed that the angle of inclination (or dip) was fixed, since pots stood level on their bases when stacked in the kiln. This may be true of glazed ware, where only the unglazed base or spurs had contact with other objects; even so, a pot may balance on its base and yet its axis be several degrees out of the vertical. But most ancient pots were not glazed and, since there was no danger of their fusing together, they could be stacked at any angle in the kiln. Tests that we made on a

few random specimens of ancient Greek pottery suggest that they were so stacked.

For this reason we decided at the beginning of our inquiry to concentrate on structures which had not been disturbed since they were fired and magnetized. The walls and bottoms of kilns have proved very satisfactory. In firing they have been subjected to a heat of not less than 800° C. Since they are commonly built in pits about 2 ft. deep, their lower parts are often well preserved, and because of their shape and nature it is fairly easy to decide whether those parts have shifted since firing. Their period of use was generally short, so that the remanent magnetization, if not that of the last firing, accumulated over only a few years. Lastly, kilns are fairly numerous in this country, especially of the Roman period, and normally several examples are excavated every year.

It appears from the above account that the application of magnetic analysis to archaeological material must have an extremely restricted scope. Unless some more widely useful method of extracting chronological data can be devised, the excavator's cherished hope of reading absolute dates in the pottery that he encounters in such profusion, and on which he so greatly depends for his chronological sequences, must remain in the insubstantial realm of dreams.

The American contribution to remanent magnetic analysis as an instrument of archaeological research has been of the slightest. The Department of Terrestrial Magnetism of the Carnegie Institution of Washington, D. C., is admirably equipped and staffed for such work; but its interests thus far have been directed toward geological rather than archaeological material, presumably because the prospects in the latter field have been judged to be unpromising.

Preliminary announcement has recently been made of an alternative method for chronological analysis of ceramic material, which is based on wholly different considerations and is not hampered by the prime obstacle besetting magnetic analy-sis—i.e., the obligation to treat only objects still exactly oriented as they were when they were fired. The new process is still in its early stages of testing and perfecting; and no extensive account of its successes or failures, its merits and inconveniences, its range and reliability, has yet been published. Lacking this ac-credited information, I have been able to gather only a rather sketchy outline for "thermoluminescent analysis."

Radiation "fall-out" is today the urgent concern of an alarmed populace dreading the damage that it may inflict upon living cells. It should be some slight reassurance to this dis-quieted multitude to learn that nuclear radiation is not a recent innovation of man's misdirected inventiveness, but has persisted unremittingly since the dawn of life on earth. It may be no more encouraging, but it is certainly more surprising, to learn further that inanimate matter also, which is subjected to the same continuous bombardment by alpha particles, has been un-dergoing radiation damage through the ages and that this dam-age cumulatively builds up to scientifically measurable propor-tions. An opportunity for archaeological dating results that is strikingly parallel to the magnetic dating of terracotta already discussed. Just as the high temperature of the potter's oven re-leases the magnetically oriented iron particles in the clay, so it simultaneously releases the strains of accumulated radiation damage in the material. And just as the particles of iron orient themselves anew to the earth's magnetic field as the clay cools, so, with all previous damage annulled by super-heating, new radiation damage to the clay will begin to build up afresh. This event introduces a measurable time-mark into the products of the kiln. I quote a brief statement of the physical situation that arises:

> [The extent of] radiation damage [accumulated since the clay was baked] can be detected by measuring the minute

amount of visible light that is emitted if the temperature is raised by several degrees centigrade; this light represents the energy released as the distortions of the crystal structure disappear. It can be measured by means of a photomultiplier. The light output is dependent not only on the time since previous heating but also on the uranium content of the clay and on the susceptibility to damage. Consequently it is necessary firstly to measure the natural alpha radioactivity of the specimen, and secondly to measure the damage produced by bombardment with a known quantity of radiation from an artificial source. [M. H. Aitken, *Physics and Archaeology* (Interscience, 1961).]

The device of thermoluminescent dating originated in geological research and is largely of American creation. The application to archaeology is credited to G. Kennedy of the University of California, who is even now actively engaged in testing and perfecting methods that—if successful—will considerably outdistance the achievements of magnetic dating, since they escape the sharp restriction to samples collected in their undisturbed state. (The ensuing total destruction of the sample cannot be considered a serious impediment, since only a small fragment is required for testing.)

It is too soon to estimate accurately the archaeological import of thermoluminescent dating. Potentially, at least, it is a chronological technique comparable in value to radiocarbon analysis.

A third, and again wholly different, analytical technique still under process of development devotes itself to an alternative aspect of ceramic antiquities by centering interest not on *time* but on *place* of manufacture. Procedure is based on the highly probable presumption that the chemical composition of ceramic ware must differ characteristically in accord with the geographic area from which its clay was extracted. A highly sensitive method of analysis capable of quantitatively determining the minute traces of the rarer mineral elements in clay might therefore serve to establish its local provenance. The fabric of ancient

Corinthian vases is so distinctively different from that of other contemporary Greek productions that even the inexperienced eye can recognize it. Since this is the case, its chemical composition cannot fail to be equally distinctive. In other Greek fabrics, for which the eye cannot thus detect provenance by mere inspection, it is reasonable to suppose that the more penetrative sight of the laboratory technician will discover less obvious, but equally significant, distinction. Even so, the clays from various beds in the same geologic region normally cannot be expected to differ so greatly in their chemical composition that the ordinary procedure of qualitative-quantitative chemical analysis will be adequate. A more minutely sensitive process is required; and this may be either the familiar method of spectroscopy or a much more novel recourse to nuclear physics. Both of these methods have been employed on ceramic samples for which archaeological controls have previously identified the centers of manufacture.

The first of these methods of analysis, using the spectroscope, depends on a routine procedure, except insofar as the exact evaluation of traces of chemical elements in very minute concentration demands certain refinements of a photometric nature, into which it is unnecessary to enter here.

The second method of ceramic analysis uses a nuclear reactor to bombard the specimen of clay with a beam of neutrons. These neutrons may be either of high or of low energies, yielding different advantages for the purpose of analysis. Using high energy neutrons, technicians note the liability of the various chemical elements to absorb selectively, i.e. to accept only those neutrons "pitched" at energies characteristic for them. Measurement of the absorption of neutrons at these various characteristic energy levels supplies the knowledge that these specific elements are present in the clay and indicates their degree of concentration, even when they are represented by extremely minute traces.

On the other hand, bombardment with *low* energy neutrons will serve to radioactivate atoms within the clay specimen. The amount of radioactivity can then be measured, thereby determining not merely what are the elements from which radio-emanation is proceeding but also the relative quantities of these elements present in the clay. As in carbon 14 analysis, the characteristic rate of radioactive decay reveals the identity of the element. The various elements are further distinguishable by the kind and energy level of the radiant particles that they emit after nuclear bombardment. It is claimed that a gamma ray spectrometer will not only count the individual particles emitted but will separate the count into groups at different energies!

All of this may seem abstruse and highly mysterious to the normally professional archaeologist; but its aura of cabalistic control over instruments of incredible precision is extremely reassuring to him. In actual operation the radioactive analysis of ceramic samples is not without its technical hurdles. The total destruction of the ceramic sample in certain procedures may be more than casually inconvenient when objects of artistic or historic worth are involved. When this is not a consideration of moment, there are still various disturbing factors, sufficient to cloud the serenity of science with the obfuscation of material accident. On this account, although in several instances the findings, when checked against information derived from other archaeological data, have been spectacular in their confirmations, it must be granted that in other cases the results have been unencouraging. Most of these new devices are still in an experimental stage.

It is not difficult to discover reasons for these lapses from success; but rather than discuss them, it may be appropriate to consider in more general terms the bearing of the present-day archaeological appeal to scientific technology so well exemplified by nuclear emission and carbon 14 analysis. The prospect for archaeology is one of revolutionary change. All the scientific aids discussed in this chapter are aimed, in one way or another, at attaching date tags to the hitherto undated and undateable material with which archaeology is vitally concerned. If such date tags can be supplied everywhere on demand, archaeology will be able to move on to its prime objective—assembling the cultural evidence for man's long rise from savagery to civilization and documenting every step correctly for time and place and evolutionary sequence.

It is a splendid ambition. With the help of modern science it now seems probable that archaeology will achieve it.

⤳ 5 ⤵

ARCHAEOLOGY AND HUMANISM

Archaeology and anthropology are so inextricably intervolved that any formal dividing line between the two will often be little more than a verbal distinction. Anthropology admits a wider interest in that it interprets socially and psychologically what archaeology presents materialistically. Restrictively, under the terms of their respective occupations, the anthropologist does not dig, the archaeologist does not make sociological interpretations. However, the two disciplines are not always or everywhere kept apart. Within the confines of the United States the anthropologist digs and the archaeologist carries on anthropological studies. The conflation is a result of the specific nature of the available material, since there is little to be dug out of North American soil except prehistoric artifacts without relevance to our present culture but often very closely related to native Indian cultures, which are, it is fair to say, anachronistic survivals from prehistoric times. Such a situation is not paralleled in culturally more highly evolved environments such as Europe or many parts of Asia. In consequence the archaeological profession in our country is rather sharply dichotomized according to the focus of interest into the anthropological archaeologists who work on native soil and the un-anthropologically oriented archaeologists active in foreign lands or concerned with their antiquities. Even the diggers of prehistoric Europe and Asia—who might be expected to share the anthropological outlook of their North American counterparts—tend to restrict themselves to the more purely archaeological aspects of their work of penetration into the past. This may result from the more or less accidental circumstance that Old World archae-

ology moved into prehistory out of history and therefore in-
stinctively treats prehistory as a prelude to civilization. The archaeological exploration of the hitherto less civilized regions of
Africa will presumably show a more anthropological approach,
undirected by historical cultural associations.

According to another distinctive definition, the archaeologist
concerns himself only with objects of relatively considerable
antiquity, while the anthropologist avails himself of the larger
opportunities for studying mankind vividly and fully in his
present-day actuality. But to say that archaeology concerns itself
only with man in the past while anthropology concentrates on
man in the present would be to erect an imaginary barrier between the two professions. It is not so much in their subject
matter as in their mental approach and intellectual emphasis
that the two disciplines draw apart. The archaeologist is a physical materialist, accepting the discovery, collection, preservation,
and restoration of material substance as his ever acknowledged
function, which he may overstep in his thinking but never ignore in his practical activity. The anthropologist will treat material objects rather as a concrete basis, a visible starting point,
for mental syntheses and constructions of cultural patterns of
human behavior and beliefs. Working at different levels, the
archaeologist may exclaim, "Behold what man has wrought!",
to which the anthropologist might rejoin, "Behold, rather, what
man IS and HOW he acts, what he senses and what he imagines."
It would be inaccurate and unjust to pretend that either of these
approaches to the study of man is more—or less—humane than
the other.

Again, it is largely the outcome of historical accident that the
archaeologist tends to claim for himself the higher and more
self-consciously aesthetic forms of art, leaving to the anthropologist its more markedly tribal or savage manifestations. The
archaeologist is naturally attracted to the more developed civilizations because these have left more varied, more intrinsically at-

tractive, more historically significant objects for him to discover, to publish, and to study. Concerning himself with these, he finds himself on common ground with the historian of art and, where a literate culture is involved, with the politico-economic historian, the philologist, and the student of literature. It is only natural that, consorting with these, he adopts their points of view. Conversely, where his attention is directed toward a less complexly evolved cultural environment, the archaeologist finds himself involved with technologically immature products and vestigial remains such as the anthropologist can best help him to interpret.

The nexus between the archaeologist and the historian of art can be even more tightly drawn.

The interplay between archaeology and art history does not hinge solely on the ability of the archaeologist to furnish the art historian with calendar dates for his use, any more than it consists only in extracting from the soil novel material for his consideration. It is true that both of these services are expected of him, and that it is in these activities that the archaeologist most signally performs his characteristic functions. But it would not be correct to insist that the archaeologist's proper domain extends no further than the digging, sorting, and chronological ordering of material mementoes of past human industry and that everything beyond the territory thus defined ceases to be his affair. There is an intermediate zone between the fields staked out by the art historian and the archaeologist—a zone not so much neutral as shared in common—in which the archaeologist aspires to become an art historian (or, alternatively, the art historian must descend to the archaeological level), much as there are overlapping domains that the archaeologist quite properly occupies in common with the political and the cultural historian, the anthropologist, and the historian of technology and science. It is in these zones of mutual contact that the archaeologist ceases to be a purely material technician and a practitioner of borrowed scientific devices (the aspect on which this essay has laid such stress) and takes on the status and responsibilities of the philosopher and the humanist.

As I have emphasized, a major task for archaeological activity is the construction of a chronological scaffolding or an encompassing temporal frame for the accumulated material with which it operates. To this end, archaeology is prone to distinguish between relative chronologies (which seek to establish only a correct sequential order of events) and absolute chronologies (which attach a calendar of astronomically precise dates to individual objects in order to anchor them firmly in historic time). But this distinction—however much it may affect methods of technical procedure and theoretic results—is not always mandatory on the archaeologist in his service to other disciplines. Political history can scarcely be written except against a background of chronicle dates; but this is not so much the case for economic history, while cultural history and the history of art may be constructed on only the barest framework of annalistic record. In these the orderly succession of phenomena, their individual scope and character, their mutual dependence and interrelation, may all be of greater interest than the exact temporal record of their occurrence. Thus, the history of European painting can be traced from two interrelated but fundamentally very different methods of approach. It can be presented as a documented chronicle of individual artists, with illustration of their works tied to the specific years in which they were active. But the same history can also be written in quite different and less individually personal terms as the evolution and diffusion of technical devices and pictorial accomplishment or again as the growth of styles and the changing arbitrament of taste. In this latter form of aesthetic history the principal centers of attention are the technical progress under physiological and psychological conditioning and the evolutionary sequence of more or less impersonal events with their accompanying influences and interrelations. Since this is a reputable and recognized form of research for the historian of art, it follows that both archaeology and art criticism are familiar with the two variant forms of artistic chronicling—the one dependent on absolute temporal documentation, the other content to operate with purely relative sequences.

The former or documentary type of individual achievement naturally attracts the art historian whenever the materials for such a type of art history exist. Understandably and justifiably, he gives his attention to the artists as individuals with distinctive personal attainments rather than submerging them in more abstract conceptions and less personal generic principles, gratuitously applying these to a sequence of events already perfectly clear to him. The archaeologist, on the other hand, is very generally confronted with an amorphous and anonymous mass of heterogeneous and fortuitously surviving objects of art. In consequence he is forced to adopt a different point of view, aimed at introducing coherent order on purely internal evidence, frequently without any assistance whatsoever from historic chronicle or other external source of information.

All mimetic (or, as it is more frequently called, representational) art is strictly conditioned by physiological and psychological factors imposed by the mechanism of vision. Because of this, the stylistic career of the imitative arts—whether sculpture or painting or other genus—is largely predetermined by controlling forces beyond the volition or invention of the executant craftsman. The artist is compelled to work within the boundaries of these restraints and in submission to their dictation, even while within their imposed directives he may possess full freedom of individual thought and action.

Classical Greek sculpture affords an excellent illustration of the working of this law of technical determinism. What might be termed the "personal" history of this art as derived from the list of its most famous masters and their most celebrated works has been recorded by ancient writers. But the Greek sculpture that has survived to our own times is almost entirely impersonal, in the sense that it is accompanied by no identifying label of individual authorship. Thanks to this impediment, although there can be no doubt that many famous masterpieces may have been preserved for us in the guise of Roman marble copies, it has been a difficult and hazardous task to equate the extant copies with their original prototypes as recorded in ancient literary sources. In order to assign our very considerable mass of surviving ancient sculpture (whether copies or original work) to its historic context of time and place, a preliminary task of no mean magnitude must first be performed. The surviving sculptures—including the great majority that cannot be identified by any artist's name—must be treated as material evidence for constructing an anonymous chronicle of Greek sculptural style through its periods of developmental change. Once the stylistic career of Greek sculptural production has been established in correct chronological sequence (and, be it added, with some understanding of the determining causes dictating this sequence!), a framework will exist for interpolating our specimens of Greek sculpture into their proper places in the series. This is a task that the art historian *might* perform, but one that the archaeologist *must* perform if he wishes to make his field of interest intelligently useful to others. As a result of the conditions under which he operates, the archaeologist has been obliged, to a much greater extent than the art historian, to cope with undated and undocumented art. Besides, chronological elucidation is one of archaeology's main preoccupations.

Since he is so frequently unsupplied with pertinent names and dates, the archaeologist has to construct anonymous and unchronicled art history. Because of the inadequacy of archaeological information derived from excavation, he has had to scrutinize the objects in and for themselves apart from any historical context and to search for some self-contained chronology of style or thematic content. At once he is confronted with a far reaching problem: Is stylistic change haphazard and capricious or is it governed by laws of its own? If the latter, is its evolutionary career uniquely individual to each separate culture and environment, or are there common trends and common phases in all mimetic art, irrespective of time, place, creed, or degree of civilization? These questions affect the intelligent understanding of art history in its widest aspect; but it is the archaeologist rather than the professed art historian who is most directly concerned with answering them.

The situation is much the same for the graphic arts. The art historian who is well supplied with factual information on individual artists and their works and has insight into the characteristic traits that distinguish these artists one from another—as is the case, for example, in Italian painting from A.D. 1200 on —is little inclined to by-pass these distinctive criteria of personality and genius in order to look behind them for generic laws dictating the course of stylistic development. Yet the more sweeping stylistic determinants exist and are effectively operative, since they are rooted in the physiology of vision and the psychology of graphic mimicry of the objective world; and it is in the elucidation of these fundamental and impersonal forces that the archaeologist in the role of philosophic humanist can make a vital contribution to the intellectual understanding of artistic phenomena.

Sir John Beazley's spectacular feat of introducing order into the thousands of surviving red-figure Attic vases by assigning them to the (for the most part nameless) painters in whose workshops they originated, may perhaps be denied status as an archaeological performance, since methodologically it differs hardly at all from the art historian's well-established practice of attributing unsigned paintings to their presumptive masters on grounds of telltale traits of individual mannerisms. In reply it may be argued that only a classicist with archaeological training and experience would have been competent to deal with this vascular material. From which it should become apparent that art history and archaeology may be closely interlocking disciplines and that there are areas of inquiry common to both, wherein differentiation between the two disciplines is largely a matter of verbal definition. It is hardly a profitable issue to draw boundaries between the two professions. "Non nobis, Domine, non nobis!" should be every true scholar's motto, since the surest promise for advance in knowledge lies in mutually tolerant (or better, cordially sympathetic) collaboration between related disciplines.

The art historian in turn can repay the archaeologist in his own coin. The career of classical Greek and Roman wall painting is singularly ill-documented, in that the literary notices correspond to no surviving specimens of the art (all major original work was destroyed long ago), while those examples that have survived are almost invariably unsigned and almost as invariably of mediocre quality. Faced with this fragmentary material, the speculative archaeologist may turn for guidance to European painting from the thirteenth century on, in order to discover the "stylistic determinants" ruling the painter's efforts and the sequential development of his technical devices and expressive forms. Having learned these, he may then turn back to classical times and, by assuming the applicability to antiquity of principles operative in subsequent ages, he may hope to introduce intelligible order where none at first sight could be described.

There are other less familiar cultural environments from which little else than the art has been salvaged, undocumented survivals from otherwise unrecorded epochs of human activity. Such—except for stray notices in ancient writers like Herodotus —is the Scythian art of the south Russian steppes and its Siberian cogeners; and such is African Negro sculpture (when it is not too recently inspired or of outright modern manufacture). To such as these, only archaeological methods of chronological determination and grouping can be applied. Similarly, the remarkable pottery of the Incas and the allied Peruvian ceramic wares cannot be sorted out and reduced to orderly sequence on any criteria of individual attribution to masters or workshops such as have been applied to Greek vases. The material context of their discovery and removal from the soil, and the study of their stylistic interrelations, their sequences of shapes and decorative modes and mimetic fidelity, are the only useful guides to chronological ordering and cultural setting. In short, archaeology is capable of constructing a history of art for cultural regions wherein art has had no history.

Arrayed against the shifting fads and fancies of contemporary interpretations of art in terms of the subconscious and the emotional traumata of the human psyche, archaeology may seem a very backward science with its insistence on material positivism and its matter-of-fact interpretations of the relics in which it deals. But for that very reason it may be a healthy influence in an emotionally disturbed society through so flatly insisting on the objective reality of man's past behavior. Its reading of the evidence that it encounters is often discouragingly commonplace and depressingly unimaginative. Thus, to cite an example beyond the purview of art history, when burials are unearthed in which the corpses have been contracted into "foetal attitude," with knees drawn up under chins, there are those who speak of symbolic re-entry into the maternal womb; whereas the excavating archaeologist, having some notion of the labor attendant on digging holes in hard and stony or perhaps tightly frozen ground, contents himself with reflecting how he too might constrict a dead body into the smallest possible compass if he were obliged to dig a hole in which to bury it!

From this derisive disbelief in the disingenuous vaporings of pseudo-scientific sentimentalists stems, perhaps, the archaeologist's unemotional outlook on art as subject to material restraints and technical determination, susceptible to rational analysis and impartial scrutiny, a phenomenon lodged in time more enduring than the transient life of its practitioners.

The relation of archaeology to political history is too familiar to demand more than passing comment. Where a continuously coherent chronology of events is already established, the archaeological contribution is apt to consist of evidence confirming or amplifying what is already known or filling lacunas where fully detailed knowledge is lacking. It is rarely that newly acquired archaeological data directly contradict or overthrow historical surmises founded on written documents, especially when these documents take the form of previously composed chronicles and epitomes. But even when a literate civilization such as that of ancient Greece or Rome has supplied the historian with a body of written material adequate for his immediate purposes, the added information derivable from inscriptions, coins, and other material documents unearthed by archaeology has proved so voluminous and so pertinent that Greek and Roman history have been rewritten almost from decade to decade in recent times in order to absorb the increase in knowledge and to re-evaluate the previously known in the light of the newly acquired information.

More drastically, if it had not been for the archaeologists who dug up the cuneiform tablets and the philologists who read and interpreted them, ancient Mesopotamian history would have remained a mere collection of classical and Biblical references to a vague and inactual civilization. Minoan Crete existed for the historian only as a shadowy retroprojection from classic legends out of which no historic actuality could be discerned until the present century's methodically pursued excavation of the preclassical Cretan palaces and towns conjured up out of oblivion an entire lost civilization of a very advanced and hitherto wholly unfamiliar type. The archaeological achievement was all the more notable through having had no support from interpretable literary documents.

The Etruscans too have been in some measure rescued from the shadowy past. Despite contemporaneous Greek and Roman sources of literate information—and not, as in the case of Minoan Crete, late legendary tradition—and native Etruscan inscriptional material in fairly considerable supply, no satisfactory comprehension of Etruscan cultural development was achieved until archaeology added its tremendous impulse.

But it is in the vast and hitherto unexploited domains of prehistory that archaeology will make its most valuable contribution to our knowledge of the past. Where the literate present impinges on the illiterate past, archaeology can widen the historical horizon by picking up the cultural record and carrying it back into the preliterate epoch. This is well illustrated in the Mayan and Incan realms, where Spanish memoirs and chronicles, eked out by a scant understanding of native tongues, carry the historian back only a few centuries to a time at which he would have to abandon his task were not archaeology at hand to open up a path into preceding periods.

What sort of cultural history will one day be written for central Africa depends almost entirely on what documents archaeological exploration will supply.

Where a prehistoric rather than a historic context is involved, the number of sites today clamoring to be dug is prodigious. This is the case partly because prehistoric time is so much longer than historic time, even as prehistoric territory extends far beyond the areas of literate historic occupation; partly it is because intelligent interest in prehistory and unhistoric cultures is of comparatively recent origin; and partly, also, it is because prehistoric man was not concentratedly urban and hence has left more widely dispersed evidence of his presence. The rather abrupt modern realization that men have had an archaeologically detectable past wherever they have raised themselves above the most frugal state of savagery has expanded archaeological enterprise from a locally restricted preoccupation with the past to a planetary undertaking of hitherto unsuspected magnitude. Granted that it may be possible to unbend some of the tenseness of national self-pride in the countries that at present suspect and resist even the least self-seeking foreign intrusion, there is a reasonable prospect that American technical resourcefulness seconded by American financial resources may bring American-bred archaeological research into worldwide leadership. In order to accomplish this, more and better training at an advanced level will have to be supplied by our institutions of learning. But the goal is a rational one; and the chances for reaching it are as good as the opportunity is great.

WESTERN ART HISTORY

⋞⋟

JAMES S. ACKERMAN

PROFESSOR OF FINE ARTS
HARVARD UNIVERSITY

PREFACE

When we were asked by the Council of the Humanities to write
these essays, it was left to us to decide whether we would discuss how our discipline had developed or how it ought to
develop. I chose the latter because it seemed more stimulating;
but toward the end of my stay in Princeton, reflecting on the
partiality of great foundations to descriptions and histories of
Things As They Are, I felt it would be ungrateful not to append
a brief survey of past and present works and personalities, and
this turned out to fit rather well with the preceding chapters. In
neither the theoretical nor the historical portion of this essay
can I represent myself as a spokesman for my colleagues; had I
restricted my statements to those I believed would be acceptable
to a majority of art historians, I should have been reduced to
mere documentation. On the contrary, everything written in the
following pages has the bias of a particular point of view that
may not be shared wholeheartedly by anybody. I have tried,
however, to set forth that point of view explicitly, so that the
reader might judge which of its biases he finds congenial.

My bibliography makes no claim to thoroughness; it indicates
a few writings that are useful in studying the principles of art
history and criticism, and includes those to which I am most
indebted for stimulus. I have gratefully benefited from the con-
versation and criticism of Ernst Gombrich, Jesse Reichek,
Meyer Schapiro, and friends at Princeton in the Council and in
the Department of Art and Archaeology, particularly Joseph
Barber, Donald Egbert, Wen Fong, Richard Schlatter, Walter
Sutton, and, of course, my collaborator in this volume.

◄§ 1 §►

THE NATURE OF ART HISTORY

As philosophy is made by philosophers, history is made by historians; the making of it is a creative activity. The "science" of history, or corpus of techniques by which we discover, verify, and analyze our data, is equally important, but it is less in need of attention at this moment. It has prospered so well on American soil that it often threatens to control rather than to serve us.

We who study the arts of the past should be especially aware of the creative component in our occupation, because our primary datum is a work of art, something that we are not quite able even to describe with clinical objectivity, supposing we should want to, and something that, as we follow its path through past generations, may be seen as the source—or the object—of the most conflicting opinions and interpretations.

Most of my colleagues, even the more "scientific" ones who would not allow that there is an art of history, agree that the work of art is the primary datum of the art historian. And because the work of art is a different sort of primary datum from that of other historians, there is a basic difference between art history and other historical disciplines—not only political-social-cultural history, but also that of other arts, particularly literature.

Like other historians, the art historian studies events that occurred in the past, but he is interested in events chiefly insofar as they help to illuminate a product—the work of art itself— that is physically present. Occasionally he tries to reconstruct lost works of art, but as a rule he studies objects made at another time but existing now, more or less in their original form; sometimes in the environment for which they were planned (e.g., as architecture) and sometimes in a newly created environment (the museum). So a work of art may be as real and as useful to us as it was to those by and for whom it was made.

When we do study the events that lead to the making of works of art, our methods are nearly indistinguishable from those of the student of political events such as elections and battles; they are wholly in the past and may be reconstructed more or less clearly by means of documents, chronicles, and the like. Indeed, when an art historian engages in the study of events for their own sake, he becomes a social historian: there is no difference in principle or in technique between a biography of Michelangelo and a biography of Luther or of Charles V, or between the publication of documents on the building of Versailles and on the War of the Spanish Succession. But events are perhaps proportionately more important to historians—witness the Greek and Latin fathers of history; to art historians they remain tools.

Since works of art are, in a physical sense, artifacts, we may get further by comparing them to what could be called political artifacts. Firearms as well as kings have affected the course of history, and other "artifacts," such as laws, constitutions, or rites, come still closer to the arts in embodying the values of individuals and societies. But most artifacts of this kind differ from works of art in that their significance is inseparable from their social function. Usually they are fashioned in response to some social need of the moment, then are used to influence the course of subsequent events, and are judged principally by the effectiveness of that influence. They are discarded or fall into permanent disuse as soon as they cease to function efficiently, like the crossbow or the Eighteenth Amendment. A technological artifact such as the crossbow cannot be evaluated apart from what it does—its effects or influence; we cannot get much from what it is, unless, as occasionally happens, it qualifies also as a work of art. By contrast, the work of art may be valued more for what it is than for what it does. It may not fulfill any specific public need ("art for art's sake") or, if it does, it may fail to function effectively in its role and still be desirable as art. (Caravaggio's altarpieces, rejected by the churches for which they were commissioned, were snapped up by collectors.) But even highly functional altarpieces, or totem poles, or drinking kylixes, survive the events and conditions that brought them into being and are preserved and enjoyed by people who might be ignorant or only dimly aware of their original purpose. Often works of art are cast aside, become unfashionable or even abhorrent, either because they have ceased to function as they were intended to do or simply because they do not conform to a prevailing standard of taste. But unlike an obsolete social artifact, a rejected work of art may excite at any moment sympathy and understanding as vivid as it did in its original historical context.

More may be said, however, of the social artifact embodying values—because, while we usually judge a law or a similar formulation just in terms of its effects, it does have meaning, like a work of art, independent of its success or failure as a social tool. Constitutions, credos, even actions of the past may be studied as documents not only of the flux of history, but of the human mind and imagination. In this way we study the writings of Galileo or Newton, not only to trace the origins of modern science but also to see how profound thinkers dealt with their environment, their problems, and their discoveries. At times, art historians do the same, in investigating the artist's reaction to his materials and tools, or to earlier and contemporary artists. So long as the artifact is a means for penetrating to the situation or to the personality of the makers, the aims of art history do not differ much from those of social or scientific history.

But this is a great reservation; the history of art is not the history of artists in the sense that social history is the history of men. The social and political historian uses the artifacts of the past in order to reconstruct in imagination a human situation that he cannot directly experience. The art historian, by contrast, uses what he can discover of past situations to supplement a direct experience of the artifact. In one process the artifact is a guide to a hypothetical reconstruction of the past; in the other the reconstruction of the past is a guide to the understanding and evaluation of the artifact. Though we do not read Newton's *Principia* to learn physics, or the Eighteenth Amendment to learn how to control the consumption of alcohol, we do visit the Acropolis at Athens and the Sistine Chapel to experience just what they have to convey. An architect or a painter might get more useable ideas from them than from more recent monuments. Note that I did not say "what Pheidias and Michelangelo have to convey," because we go to Greece or Rome to experience the monument, not the man, though we may be encouraged by a taste for his individual style. Indeed, one measure of the value of a work of art is the degree to which its message is universally meaningful and not restricted to the particular conditions and desires that brought it into being. Whereas we understand Newton to the degree that we understand what he intended to say and why, we may understand a work of art in ways that never occurred to its author, and conversely, we may find his actual intentions entirely irrelevant, or even embarrassing. The value and significance of works of art are not diminished or necessarily altered by cultural changes and the passage of time; they have meaning independent of their creators and social origins in a way that other kinds of human creations do not have.

Because of this difference, works of art produced in the past may be experienced without historical consciousness; since much of their meaning is unrelated to the date or circumstances of their origin, the Acropolis and the Sistine Chapel can move visitors entirely innocent of Greek or Renaissance culture. This does not mean that the intervention of the historian is of no account; through his efforts art is drawn from obscurity, its original form and place is revealed; but above all, knowledge of its provenance, authorship, traditions, and the like is made available to those who want to embrace perspectives other than that of a parochial mid-twentieth century observer. But historical knowledge of itself does not suffice to promote aesthetic experiences, which is why the arts are the subject of criticism as well as of historical research.

Since fundamental values in the work of art are inaccessible to historical method, the historian must be a critic as well. I do not mean to discredit the use and interpretation of works of art primarily as documents and catalysts of social and intellectual activity, but practiced rigorously, this method becomes a kind of political and social history, not the history of art. As long as the work of art is studied as a historical document it differs from the archival document only in form, not in kind. The art historian should be interested in the difference in kind, which is immanent in the capacity of art to awaken in us complex responses that are at once intellectual, emotional, and physical, so that he needs, in addition to the tools of other historians, principles and methods specifically designed to deal with this unique mode of experience. Providing we create a philosophical framework built upon this special nature of art, the techniques and the discoveries of social history or of any other historical or scientific discipline can only enrich our experience. Conversely, the history of art may enrich other historical disciplines not only by discovering artifacts that help to define historical structures (particularly for civilizations, such as those of ancient Mesopotamia or Crete, whose chronology we know almost exclusively from art) but by a communication with human feeling in the past of a sort that can be suggested through penetrating criticism.

The dual existence of the work of art as a document of the past and as an object in the present brings to mind the duality of experience we encounter in a museum. Here we find ourselves face-to-face with actual objects of many past eras, but we see them as coexisting all at the same moment. Without specialized information that is not provided by the objects themselves, there is no way that we can see them as products of a greater or lesser antiquity; even the expert in charge of an exhibit may be unable, for lack of historical or archaeological data, to arrange his objects in a proper chronological order. Still, we may be profoundly moved by them, and at this moment it may seem, indeed, as if the past history of the objects were a matter of no importance except to scholars. A like situation cannot be conceived in the experience of past political or social actions, which rarely reward study apart from the context in which they occurred. But, while the nature of the work of art makes it meaningful even in a historical and spatial vacuum, the isolation is an extreme situation that is likely to restrict one's experience and understanding severely. Nobody seriously recommends historical innocence except for polemic purposes.

I set the scene for dramatizing the presentness of past art in a museum because there in particular history is violated. Not only has the artistic achievement of all mankind been distilled into a sequence of galleries, but each of the single works has been drawn out of the environment for which it was conceived and has been placed in another, historically neutral and spatially meaningless. Seeing the Parthenon sculptures in their vast hangarlike hall in the British Museum is not like seeing those that remain on the Acropolis. In the museum they are a collection of pieces of sculpture that, as we read on the label, were made in the fifth century B.C. in Athens; on the Acropolis they belong to that magnificent ensemble of architecture and nature for which they were designed, and they are illuminated by the sunlight under which they were carved. There—providing the observer is moderately well informed—history becomes vitally enmeshed in his perceptions, and it plays a vastly different part than the museum label. The same is true of the Byzantine mosaics in Ravenna, or a Renaissance altarpiece seen on the altar of a medieval church. The art that suffers least loss in the museum is that made for collectors rather than commissioned for a particular function and place. In recent centuries an increasing proportion of art has been of this kind; it blossomed with Renaissance private collections and helped to form the taste that made our museums possible. Surely the fact that we are used to looking at modern paintings and sculptures as if they belonged nowhere in particular makes it easier for us to treat the arts of older civilizations that way too.

We might expect the deracination caused by museums (and still more by photography which, as Malraux put it, creates a "museum without walls") to discourage all interest in historical perspective and to promote a kind of sensual aestheticism. But the opposite has occurred: as more works of art were removed from their intended surroundings, more effort was made to recreate conceptually their physical and cultural context. The rise of the public museum was accompanied by the rise of scholarship in the arts, and in this country the museum changed from a repository to an educational institution. While museums greatly reduce a sense of the original temporal and spatial differences among works of art, they paradoxically promote the historical approach by bringing objects together in one place and by exhibiting them in conditions that are uniform and favorable for study. So we may say of the Parthenon sculptures that the "proper" way to see them—on the Parthenon—gives a less clear and comfortable impression than the exhibit in London where, contrary to the original intention, they are accessible to close examination.

The persistence of historical curiosity in the museum age demonstrates that the distinction between looking at works of art only for their expressive powers or only as documents of history is artificial. It is improper to speak of two distinct ways of looking at art; we look as whole persons and, if we know some-

133

thing about what we are looking at, our knowledge colors our reaction.

Works of art of the past are distinguished from political-social acts or artifacts by their capacity to communicate independently of the conditions in and for which they were made, and by their ability to involve us emotionally and physically. Since this is true of all the arts, a further distinction must be made between the history of the spatial arts (architecture, painting, sculpture, etc.) and the history of literature and music.

The spatial arts are practiced in media that have a permanent physical reality, while other arts are not. Music and literature may be translated into physical signs—notes and words—that can be inscribed or printed on a material surface such as paper, but these signs are a key to the work of art, not the work itself. It does not matter in evaluating the work whether that key is in the hand of the author or another, or printed handsomely or poorly. It is merely a practical contrivance for securing a certain degree of permanence, and one that is not essential to the vitality or continuity of those arts. For the greater part of human history, music and poetry were preserved only by memory.

The spatial arts are not so abstract; they can be preserved only in the form and material in which they first are made, and they never are quite divorced from the matter of which they are composed and from the environment in which they are placed, or which (in the case of architectural interiors, and the design of towns and gardens) they control. It is not the rich texture of the glass that makes the windows of Chartres Cathedral great works of art; nonetheless, the quality of this physical characteristic is inseparable from the experience of the windows, and cannot be translated into another medium or even reproduced in the same medium by modern technology. I choose windows because they most vividly illustrate the fact that the spatial arts often are involved inextricably with the environment. What would they be without the sunlight, which not only enables us to see the windows (at night they are black) but also makes it possible for the windows to transfigure the illumination of the church so that beams of light themselves become the materials of art?

There is no way to reproduce a work of spatial art. In attempting to do so, one creates either another quite unique work of art (as great painters have done in making what we call replicas of their work), or a mere record that preserves certain characteristics of the work as a reminder of its over-all character. The commonest records of this kind are photographs and architectural diagrams. Though on first thought they may seem comparable to musical scores or printing, they actually are incapable of recording more than a certain restricted range of characteristics of the original work. It is sufficient to note the absence of the third dimension in photographs of sculpture and architecture; the elimination or distortion of the color of paintings; the incapacity to differentiate textures; and finally the destruction of scale to a point at which handbooks illustrate the Sistine Chapel at the same size as the miniatures of an illuminated Book of Hours made to fit a pocket. The original and the photographic copy are separated by a distance greater than that separating literary works from translations into different languages.

The validity and accuracy of the photograph as a record of an original work of art is inconstant; it varies according to the medium of the object and, within media, according to style. Engravings and woodcuts suffer least, perhaps, because they are themselves produced for multiple reproduction and are better adapted than other media to the technical limitations of photography. "Linear" paintings suffer less than "painterly" ones— Raphael and Picasso less than Titian and Monet. Sculpture and architecture are especially vulnerable to an irrelevant factor:

the photographer's taste and knowledge, which is brought to bear particularly on his choice of viewpoint, his use of natural and artificial light, and the degree to which he is tempted to make his photograph a work of art rather than a document.

It is the factor of the uniqueness and irreproduceability of works in the spatial arts that differentiates the practice of art history and criticism from that of other historical activities, and in this narrow sense allies it to those sciences that operate with unique data collected in the field, such as anthropology, paleontology, and archaeology.

So art historians are perforce travelers, but only a portion of their scholarship can be done in the field. Motion is not conducive to meditation. What is gathered in travels must be assimilated in the study, and here photographs, plans, and the like prove to be an incomparable aid, in spite of their distortions. By means of reproductions a record of works scattered around the earth may be gathered in one place for comparison; probably we learn more by the method of comparison than by any other—it is the basis of any concept of style. Photographs preserve works that have been lost or altered, and in the latter case can serve to bring us closer to the original than the experience of it in its present state. Finally, the photographer or the architectural draughtsman often bring into the study a record that is partly or wholly inaccessible to the eye under normal conditions; without such aids we should never find out what the crown of a Gothic spire really looks like, or what Michelangelo painted in the small medallions of the Sistine ceiling. Though historians sometimes muster the agility or daring to climb dizzying heights, they cannot compete with the scaffolds, the telescopic lenses, and other such technical aids that make many photographs possible.

I often envy the literary scholar who sits by his fireside with his new volume of poetry (which he has purchased at the corner bookstore) and comes as close to Chaucer or to Ariosto as it is possible to get in our time. If I want to see a fresco by a contemporary of Ariosto, I must travel thousands of miles, while to get command of the easel paintings and drawings of the same artist, I may have to visit twenty cities on two continents. But there is a compensation; as I hold one of those drawings in hand, I see it as I should have seen it in the artist's studio 450 years ago; it speaks more vividly than the new volume of Chaucer, which accurately records Chaucer's words, but not his pronunciation or the speed, rhythms, and inflections with which he meant them to be spoken. In the drawing, all the comparable nuances are preserved, because pronunciation, rhythm, and the like are idiosyncracies of personality and style that are lost in a printed poem but the equivalents of which are preserved in the characteristic line, stroke, shading, and other aspects of the drawing to which we refer when we speak of the artist's "hand."

This distinction can be made because, unlike a poet or composer, a draughtsman and more obviously a sculptor creates a *physical* form as well as an aesthetic form as he works. Part of our experience in seeing his work is a sense of his command of his raw materials and of their reciprocal authority over him. By his technique he gives them a form and a quality, yet by their physical composition they assert their own being. This tension or equilibrium between the vision of the artist and the reality of the material and technique can be experienced vividly in a Gothic cathedral, where that vision forces stone to the utmost limits of its structural potential. In the spatial arts, we enjoy not only the artist's mastery of nature, but nature itself—the crystalline quality of Pentelic marble, the richness of gold leaf in a Bible illumination, the brilliance or the patina of bronze.

The physical reality of the spatial arts makes for complexity; nature is prolific with its materials, and one artist may work with media so diverse in character that it becomes difficult to detect common traits of personality in two of his works, even in media as close as chalk and pen drawings on paper.

We say of a writer, too, that he has a "craft" or a "technique" but we mean something quite different. Though we can trace his personal imprint in the manipulation of words and phrases, these "raw materials" are man-made, and bring with them distinct connotations. Language is symbolic, not physical, and writers do not "handle" it manually in the way sculptors chisel and polish stone. So the manipulation of words is comparable to the artist's manipulation of symbols (e.g., the halo, the madonna and child) rather than of materials.

The study of physical materials and techniques of manipulating them is foreign to literary or musical history as certain problems of bibliography and notation are foreign to art history; but this comparison is misleading if we take it to mean only that every art has its own language. The physical existence of the spatial art is a *dimension* that does not exist in other arts. So there are factors of style in the spatial arts to which nothing in literature or music can be fairly compared: the choice of materials (a sculptor selects alabaster rather than marble for a figure); the choice of tools (a draftsman selects a brush rather than a pen to apply his ink); the attitude toward known methods of wielding the tools (a painter decides to accentuate rather than to hide his body movements in applying his pigment).

It is in another dimension—one that is less physical and more of the imagination—that style in the spatial arts is comparable to literary and musical style: that of the ordering of component elements (colors, bricks, notes, words) into coherent structures or compositions. On this level we can make comparisons among the several arts (Bernini's versus Crashaw's concept of the vision of St. Teresa; harmony in Renaissance music and architecture).

Art historians always have been more preoccupied with problems of style than have literary historians and musicologists, who have turned to us for a vocabulary (e.g., *Gothic, Mannerism, Baroque*). The main reason is that distinctions of style are the principal means of determining the time and place of origin of most works of art. Another reason is that the artist's "language," like the musician's, is less clearly defined than the poet's; since it is not used outside of art, society exercises less control over it—in recent painting and sculpture often no control at all. Furthermore, it is not by its nature divisible, as the Italian language is from the German, into distinct spheres. At one moment it may be international, at another moment local, and it may change radically and rapidly, forcing the observer to learn to read anew. For this reason the history of art is especially preoccupied with relationships between the language or conventions of style used in a group, nation, or era and the individual contribution of an artist or a single work, and further with the processes by which the conventions are altered.

We find a more obvious contrast between literary and art historical scholarship in the relative importance assigned to historical and to critical activity. A large number of literary scholars can be called critics; and a growing number of literature courses in American universities are designed to teach criticism. But American art historians, even those who practice some criticism in their work, rarely regard themselves as critics and rarely set themselves problems that could be called primarily critical. Courses in "appreciation" of art are offered in some universities, but the subject is considered to be suitable only for beginners and beneath the dignity of scholars. Almost all further instruction is offered in the historical context by era (Medieval Art, Renaissance Art) and/or nation (Greek Art, Italian Renaissance).

The exclusion of criticism from institutions of higher education has meant that it can be practiced professionally only in the popular press, and this has caused a virtual extinction of responsible criticism. The many "little magazines," which are more or less free of public pressures, are devoted to literary and social criticism; they are not known to be hostile to art critics, but simply cannot find enough of them. The journals devoted to painting and sculpture are primarily news magazines; those devoted to architecture are professional organs.

In practice it is easy to tell the difference between critics and historians, whether of art or of literature, but, since the distinction is somewhat artificial, it is hard to define clearly. No critic can operate without historical knowledge and historians make critical judgments every time they choose one work rather than another to illustrate a point. When art historians say that they are not critics they mean that their criticism normally is exercised on the work of art as a product of the past and stops short of issues raised by its meaning in the present. So standard art history practices critical commentary on the use of materials and techniques, on conventions of form and symbolism that constitute the style of an era or cultural group, and on traits of individual style, but rarely is concerned with the problem of defining the unique qualities of single works of art. It is the latter activity that commonly is called criticism, while the former is classified as an aspect of historical method.

Because of the great antiquity of literary history and philology and the great number of scholars engaged in those fields, students are faced with fewer major unsolved problems; historical research in the major works of English literature appears to have a constantly narrowing future. In the history of art, major figures and monuments—some entire epochs—are still indistinct; there are few artists of the past on whom we could pursue critical studies in the confidence that the work assigned to them was all actually theirs. But while these conditions explain why art historical research is particularly challenging, they do not account for the rarity of criticism; Europe, despite the same historical limitations, has consistently produced critics. We may come closer to an answer by recalling that the roots of American scholarship in art are to be found in classical archaeology; a discipline that nineteenth century Americans did not learn in the field, or even in the museums, but in libraries, as an adjunct to the study of classical literature. Another tradition, repre-sented by Charles Eliot Norton and Andrew Jackson Jarves in the nineteenth century, in which the history of art was taught as an adjunct to ethics or simply to the gentlemanly life, offered no stimulus to either criticism or scholarship, though echoes of it survived until quite recently in American universities.

In one sense, the bookish archaeologist and the gentleman amateur were produced by the same condition: America's dis-tance from the sources of all but American art. We are limited by the fact that—except in a few metropolitan centers—our libraries are better than our museums; most young Americans see works of art only in reproductions. The past association of art with gentility was due largely to the fact that only the rich could afford to travel. Today, while our major museums chal-lenge those of Europe, and more of us can get abroad, it still is not possible to become a true connoisseur (as distinct from a scholar) of European or Asian art without spending more time abroad than is feasible for most of us. Geographical distance has prompted students and scholars to seek from works of art only that information conveyed by photographs, and this means avoiding those qualities that can be found only in the original—qualities essential to criticism and connoisseurship.

The "scientific" attitude fostered by archaeological origins was reinforced in the present generation by the arrival in this country of a group of pre-eminent European teachers—mostly in the 1930's,—who were masters of empirical method. They proved to be an essential factor in the maturation of American art history, and helped to raise it to a position at the core of the humanities. It is hard to characterize the contribution to method of minds so individual and diverse as these, except to say that many have not been concerned with art as a form of experience in the present and have imparted a suspicion of critical evalua-tion. This limitation not only is consciously cultivated; it is the cornerstone of a comprehensive view of the history of art as an aspect of the history of culture—a view that tends to minimize the peculiar characteristics of art discussed in this chapter. Though splendidly practiced by its initiators, the principles as interpreted by followers often have turned rather to an arid accumulation of learning than to a search for meaning. I have great respect for the masters and differ with them only in the hope that their disciples may equal their achievement by exploiting realms into which they did not enter.

The philosophy of art history of the last generation could be called antiphilosophical; it taught nonintervention, not only in the sense of avoiding value judgments, but in the sense of minimizing the factor of creativity in historical scholarship. Its belief in the possibility of objectivity led to the conviction that history was not made but discovered, so that one needed method, intelligence, even imagination, but not a credo. Until quite recently, no American had contributed to the theory of art history (except Berenson, an entirely Europeanized American, whose attempt is anyhow unsystematic). For these reasons, I have spoken of criticism and philosophy in the same breath; criticism can become a function of art history only within a philosophical system that allows the historian a creative and evaluative role.

While literary studies had a philological and partly classical origin too, they were humanized by a long tradition of criticism sustained by distinguished writers; it is obviously an advantage to literary studies that the art and the criticism is practiced in a common medium. But even the brilliance of that tradition might not have served to admit the critic into higher learning if criticism had not, in the hands of T. S. Eliot and others of his generation, exhibited a respect for and control of historical techniques (not always exhibited however by the "new critics" who acknowledged Eliot's leadership). They showed how it was possible to consider problems of value without abandoning science.

While criticism of the spatial arts and especially of those of the past is not practiced by scholars for its own sake, it does emerge, as we should expect, in the finest historical studies, as it does in equivalent historical studies of literature. But so long as it exists as an occasional embellishment to scientific research, criticism and its problems will not be faced and cannot be solved. The scientific bias has made it possible for art history to be taught and practiced as if it were a documentary and not a creative activity. I look on criticism not as an additional technique to be adopted by historians but as a challenge that forces us to re-examine the fundamental philosophical principles by which we operate.

2

THE HISTORIAN AS CRITIC

We overhear an argument between a critic and a historian of art; the critic says "You are interested only in facts about works of art and not in quality; you approach it as a document of civilization rather than the creation of an individual spirit." The historian replies "You are so preoccupied with your own reactions that you cannot see it in its proper perspective; you are not concerned with the facts, and what you write is not criticism but inferior literature." The critic mumbles something about "dry objectivity," the historian something about "sloppy subjectivity," and they part, the one bearing with him the object, the other its qualities. Between them they have torn it apart, body from soul, as they might say. They are not the most inspired representatives of their profession, and we trust that their betters will put it back together again; but even they might be able to collaborate in that reconstruction if they were not so bemused by their rigid and rather old-fashioned concepts of subjectivity and objectivity.

The isolation of art history from art criticism in recent times is due largely to a conviction that a clear distinction can be made between facts and feelings about works of art, that we make sound "objective" observations at one moment and unreliable "subjective" evaluations at another. The separation is grounded in an outmoded psychology of perception that entirely isolates the work of art (object) from the observer (subject) by assuming the latter to be the passive recipient of emanations from the former. Thus, certain stimuli are attributed to the object and regarded as "real"—fit subject for scientific investigation—while the effect of these stimuli in the subject are attributed to individual emotions and are regarded as ephemeral and unworthy of scholarly attention. The argument is wrong because we cannot distinguish clearly "objective" from "subjective" factors in visual perceptions, and because nearly every conclusion we make about works of art bears the stamp of our personality, experience, and system of values, though in varying degrees.

We cannot say with certainty of the object that it conveys a particular message to the subject because we know that every subject gets a somewhat different message. The subject, in receiving his message, is not a sponge absorbing an invariable signal issuing from the source, but a contributing agent who sees in any object—whether or not it is a work of art—what his experience predisposes him to expect and to receive, and what his imagination prompts him to add or to alter. Therefore, what a work of art communicates can be described only in terms of an interaction between an object and a subject; it communicates nothing at all unless someone is there to look at it. In other words, there are no aesthetic objects, only physical objects, which, when observed, are capable of stimulating an aesthetic *event*.

This process may be clarified by a tautology; since our responses to visual objects are entirely within us, all of them are "subjective." On the sole basis of our own experience of the objects, we cannot designate some of our responses as "objective." But in making *statements about* responses, we distinguish as "objective" those that we believe will correspond with the experience of other people—provided they understand our premises and are supplied with the relevant information. In other words, we do not know intuitively what is objective; we learn it from our experience of the way others in our culture articulate their responses; and, as the term *objective* implies, we assume that when people proceeding on similar premises and information make or are willing to accept the same statement about some feature of an object, this feature is an inherent characteristic of that object.[1] So subjectivity and objectivity are not different, much less polar states of mind, traceable to distinct portions of the brain and separated in our experience; perceptions are complex wholes that cannot be divided neatly into categories. But communication is greatly facilitated if we use these concepts to estimate what statements will be more readily communicable (objective) and what statements—those dependent on individual experience and sensitivity—will be less readily communicable (subjective).

Criticism, then, like other forms of communication, could be thought of as an attempt to objectify subjective responses. In criticism we try to induce others to perceive works of art as we do, and the problem is simplified by our prediction that one sort of statement, which can be made in conventional terms, will be taken as relatively "objective" ("This building is thirty feet high and is made of brick"), while another demands more refined gifts of exposition and an audience capable of responding to them ("This is one of the most powerful of Rembrandt's portraits"). Statements about responses that cannot be communicated or shared by others ("This picture reminds me of my mother," or the esoteric metaphors of much contemporary critical journalism) are more relevant to autobiography or literature than to criticism; they convey information about the critic, not the work of art.

Let us think of critical practice in terms of a spectrum extending from the most readily communicable statements to those that are the most individualized and difficult to transmit. At one end of the spectrum we represent the work of art as an object to be examined in terms of its physical properties, ma-

[1] For a statement to be "objective" it must be acceptable in the cultural context in which it is made, though it need not be true. "The sun moves about the earth" was an objective statement before 1550 but not after. It would still be objective to an aborigine, who proceeds on different premises and more restricted information.

146

terials and the techniques used to make it; at the other we represent the work as a unique experience that demands the greatest powers of understanding and communication. Somewhere between these two we may place statements referring to the formal and symbolic structure (e.g., composition and subject matter) of the work—its conventional character—which we examine by analyzing conventions shared by groups of artists or characteristic of the work of single artists. Statements about physical character generally are called empirical; those about conventional character analytic, and those about the total import of the work of art intuitive or valuative. Such distinctions, however, are justifiable only as a means of classifying types of discourse; they do not define separate areas of experience. In our perception of works of art the response to size, materials, color, composition, meaning, mood and quality comes as a complex whole, not as the accumulation of distinct percepts. Indeed, any single aspect of a work of art tends to function in isolation quite differently from the way it functions in the total context. Therefore, while it is convenient to develop differentiated means of speaking of particular aspects of a work of art, the work can be represented ultimately only as a totality that corresponds to our total experience of it. It can be understood only partially by scholarship that represents it simply in terms of its more communicable aspect or by criticism that represents simply its more affective and individualized aspects.

For purposes of identification and classification we represent works of art in terms of physical properties such as size, shape, and materials. Statements about such characteristics are the most easily communicable because they can be referred to readings from conventional instruments that everyone agrees to accept as standards of measurement. Some of these—such as the record of dimensions—may come as near to perfect communicability as human beings can get, but they are few. In a catalog of drawings, for example, each entry starts with a statement of the dimensions of the sheet, the material of which it is composed, the tools and media used in making the drawing, and the incidence of identifying clues such as watermarks on paper or the identification stamps put on by earlier collectors. But, while the first of these data may come near to being free of individual variation, since they require no more than attentive readings from a calibrated scale, the others are increasingly open to interpretation. The limits of empirical description are indeterminate; the cataloger's desire to support an impression that the drawing is extremely precious, or perhaps that it is a copy, may prompt him to read an unclear clue in whatever way will suit his argument. There are no data so self-evident that they cannot be influenced by an unconscious invasion of will.

The classification of objects according to their physical properties usually is not regarded as an aspect of criticism, but it is not really a separable function. The very properties defined in this way may excite a response that is quite inaccessible to empirical measurement. Though we are unlikely to be moved by reading the dimensions of a drawing in a catalog, they symbolize proportions that can affect our response to the work when we actually see it; physical properties may be a substantial factor in our appreciation of objects made of precious stones and metals, or in techniques such as mosaic, enamel, the glazing of oil pigments, or stained glass; even common materials may awaken affective associations in a particular culture—most of us are attracted by thatched roofs and cobblestones. Whether the pleasure we get from these natural or manufactured charms can be attributed to the enjoyment of art rather than the influence of personal taste depends on whether the artist does anything to promote it. In any case it is like most physical pleasures, accessible to nearly everyone without the exercise of much effort.

Physical properties are relevant to criticism in another way. The critic's knowledge of the physical potentialities of the materials employed in any work of art must be sufficient to acquaint him with the problems they pose to the artist (e.g., the strength of marble in tension and compression is relevant to a discussion of the design of Greek temples). Furthermore, the physical condition of works of art—their present state in relation to their original state—is always relevant to interpretation. Sometimes condition can be determined by the naked eye; but laboratory techniques and historical documents often are a necessary preamble to responsible criticism. A typical example is the detection of the later repainting of old pictures by X-ray and cleaning or by reference to the history of pigment media, to contemporary reproductions and literary descriptions.

A technique usually is harder to classify and define than the materials it employs; when we examine a mural we may be sure that it is done with earth pigments in a binding medium on plaster, but not always sure that the technique is fresco (painted on wet plaster) rather than secco (painted on dry plaster); the ink and paper of a print are easily classified, but we may mistake an etching for a drypoint. Techniques, though they may remain more or less the same for millennia and in diverse cultures (e.g., the throwing of ceramic pottery on wheels), are the inventions of man and are subject to change at will, as materials are not. We can therefore speak of the history of a technique. Although techniques are more variable than materials, they are less variable than the formal or symbolic conventions of style, and for this reason are more difficult to objectify than the former and less than the latter. Domes built on pendentives, engraved gems, or cast bronze statues are found in many cultures and in arts of diverse styles; techniques are more stable than forms and symbols because they are involved in the entire technology of a society, and are less subject to variation by individual choice. Radical shifts of style often take place without changes in technique (e.g., in fresco painting) but rarely do radical shifts of technique fail to accompany changes in style. New tools suggest new forms, as is obvious in the art of recent times from steel frame skyscrapers to paintings executed with plastic paint dripped from cans. Conversely, the artist's vision of a new form stimulates the development of a new technique, as in Romanesque times, when the desire to vault churches stimulated the revival of skilled masonry work. In general, the artist is more likely to anticipate the technology in less industrialized societies; but in all art there is a close link between technical means and artistic end.

Later in this chapter I suggest that there are certain conventions of formal organization and symbolization characteristic of the style of a time and place, and comparable individualized conventions characteristic of the style of individual artists. The same may be said of technique. When we speak of "a" technique, we mean the accepted modus operandi with certain tools and materials (it also may be necessary to define the stage in the development of this technique). When we speak of "Rembrandt's technique," we mean the particular artistic personality which that individual reveals in manipulating the standard tools. In this sense, a technique, such as etching, is never the same in different hands; Rembrandt's etching technique differs significantly from that of his contemporary Seghers. Critical representation of the individualized aspect of technique draws us far from empirical discourse. To discuss it at all, we need a substantial knowledge of the range of potentialities offered by that technique, as well as a sensitivity to the nuances of style in the artist. Statements about technique in this sense demand much more of the critic and of his audience than those I have discussed so far.

Techniques, like materials, may be pleasing or displeasing in themselves; some people prefer engravings to paintings, some like the way sculptors leave the imprint of their touch on clay, or the way architects expose the bracing in half-timber buildings. The expression of such preferences seldom constitutes responsible criticism because they are imposed upon and not stimulated by particular works of art. But when the artist handles his techniques in such a way that our attention is drawn to them and we are forced into an unfamiliar response (early twentieth century collage was a shocking revision of the relation of technique to form and content), then our reaction is relevant to the particular work and therefore to criticism.

Communication of the symbolic and formal structure of works of art already is a more complex task than the exposition of physical character and technique. Ordinarily we can identify the subject matter of a figurative work of art with so little conscious effort that the process seems to be as self-evident as the measurement of size and shape. We are unaware of the substantial contribution we must make out of our own experience before we can call a configuration of red, ochre, white, and black oil pigments on canvas surface the head of a woman, or when we say that behind this head is an expanse of distant hills. We just forget to say or to think that the artist has arranged his materials in accordance with certain conventions that—providing we also are familiar with them—make it possible for us to realize the illusion of a woman's head and of a three-dimensional spatial extension related to that "head." Only when the formal conventions used or invented by the artist are *unfamiliar* to the observer (that is, when the observer is not trained to contribute to an illusion) is he likely to see a picture in terms of the configuration of pigments on a surface. Under these circumstances, he becomes aware of the differential between the physical and the communicative character of the work. Today, through museums, photography, and the press, sophisticated observers have been trained in so many conventions that they rarely lack the key to an unfamiliar work. But not long ago there were many earnest amateurs who could not perceive the head or the bottles in Cubist portraits and still lifes. In time the grammar of Picasso and Braque became so familiar that the same observers could "read" the pictures even if they did not comprehend what they had read. I speak of grammar and of reading because I think of the conventional aspect of style as a means of communication, a kind of language, within which symbolic and formal conventions are organized into coherent constructs similar to a grammar. To be able to apprehend the import of a work of art, whether it be a painting or a poem, we must first learn its language.

But knowing how to "read" the language is only a first step; it is not equivalent to understanding what is said in that language. As we pass from the measurement of physical characteristics to the decipherment of the language—from empirical to analytical exposition—we arrive at a stage that requires more learning and experience but not necessarily more critical skill or sensitivity. We may call this the province of linguistic analysis, and go on to examine two aspects of it: the interpretation of symbolic and of formal conventions.

Symbols cannot be divorced from their form either in creating or in experiencing a work of art, and the separation of "form" from "content" has caused confusion in criticism. But so long as we are speaking of conventions the distinction not only is permissible but necessary for description, because the life of symbols and the life of forms has not been everywhere coexistent in history. Some symbols (such as those for the Holy Ghost or the Virtues and Vices) pass through varied forms, while formal conventions (such as those of late antique sculpture or Gothic manuscript illumination, which were used for pagan and Christian themes alike) are applied to symbols of different, even conflicting significance.

Formal conventions are those that govern the use of the sense stimuli available within a medium and a technique (color, shape, texture, line, light-and-dark relationships) and the disposition of those stimuli according to a certain structure or relationship (composition, scale, interval, proportion). Techniques and materials impose their own limitations that become channeled into conventions (most notably in architecture, which is dependent on a technology not wholly controlled by the architect). The over-all range of color, stroke, or of compositional scheme in painting becomes fixed in conventions; a complex of such conventions constitutes the formal component of style. The great artist is often a maker—and the lesser artist a taker—of conventions, but even he most often works with reference to an established practice. And, while his innovations may effect one aspect of it—perhaps even its over-all shape—they do not sweep away the edifice. Much of today's abstract art, for example —despite its apparent antihistoricism—is done with pigments on rectangular canvases of a Renaissance scale and proportion, or is cast in traditional bronze or plaster according to ancient techniques; and even the artists who seem to be the most licentious work consistently, even rigorously, within self-imposed criteria.

The fact that a picture induces in us the illusion of a woman in a landscape we owe to our ability to grasp certain conventions: in an Egyptian fresco, we might distinguish a woman from a man by skin color; in a Greek vase, a single tree alongside the woman might imply a landscape; even the linear and aerial perspective that suggests depth in a Renaissance landscape is a convention that we must learn to interpret.

Symbolic conventions are effective when the artist and the observer share the association of a particular concept with a particular form. They may be established for any aspect of human experience that is susceptible to visual symbolization. Obviously this means that they are competent to convey far more complex meanings than "woman" and "landscape." In most art of past ages the identity of the woman would have been an essential feature of the symbolism. If she represented the Virgin Mary, a particular patrician lady, or a character from a poem, the observer's understanding of the picture's import would depend in part upon his knowledge of the religious significance of the Virgin, or the social and historical milieu of the sitter, or the narrative in the poem. Symbolic conventions, that is, can be imposed upon or sought out by the artist from the symbolic activities of civilized man other than those of the spatial arts.

As the artist combines components of formal conventions such as color and texture into a composition, so he combines isolated symbols (a virgin, halo, throne, angels, a child) into a structure of meaning. (For example, in a "santa conversazione" the Virgin and Child are shown enthroned and flanked by a small company of saints and angels.) If the artist is to convey a narrative he may need conventions not only for relating the dramatis personae one to another and to a specific setting but for suggesting temporal as well as spatial relationships (the action represented on the left may "precede" the one represented on the right; a figure may be "moving" from left to right); or even temporal-spatial ones as in the "simultaneous" representation of different views of one object in Cubism.

Reference to Cubism calls to mind the fact that symbolic conventions, far from being restricted to illusionistic representations like the lady in the landscape, are even more apparent in so-called abstract art. *Abstract* is an imprecise term; *all* symbolic conventions are abstract; we use the word simply to define art in which the conventions are not designed to produce an illusion of the common-sense world. In Cubism or in Byzantine art the conventions are rooted in objects of everyday experience, and in much of contemporary art they are not. But we cannot say that nonobjective art is without symbolic conventions, because that would mean that its language conveyed no meaning, that it was mere gibberish. The symbols of nonobjective art also refer to everyday experience; not to the experience of physical matter but of space, tension, lightness and darkness, rhythm, gesture and other incorporeal percepts. Since these experiences are not identified with fixed forms in the world of nature, the conventions for symbolizing them must be learned entirely from the art itself. That there are such conventions and that they are part of a structure as clear as in any art of the past is indicated by the fact that the styles of contemporary art are as distinct and as recognizable as those of the past. The symbolism of these artists, like that of many contemporary poets and novelists, is often personal; but when it is effective it is because the artist provides in his work the clues to its decipherment; his language then becomes a public language. Rarely in the arts today does a familiarity with the symbolic conventions from religion, poetry, or history contribute, as it has in the past, to our comprehension. We may bring our knowledge of Christianity to bear upon the "reading" of a crucifixion, but the conventions of abstract art are made only by artists.

Just as materials and techniques may be enjoyed for their own sake, so may conventions. We can like Japanese prints or idyllic landscapes generically, be fascinated with the story of the prodigal son, or prefer nonobjective art. I suppose a majority of the pictures on the walls of American homes were bought because the owners like or are accustomed to their formal or symbolic conventions, or because a certain prestige accrues to the art that exemplifies whatever conventions the social milieu may prize. In other words, those pleasures that derive from conventions define taste or fashion and, since they are excited by works of art irrespective of their individual quality, tend to be volatile.

As the linguist studies basic elements (phonemes, words) and their combination in complex structures (syntax, grammar), the critic studies colors, symbols, or architectural orders, and their combination into compositions, stories, or buildings. The method is analytic; it demands more experience and learning than the description of physical character, but less than the synthetic or evaluative criticism required for the exposition of the individualized aspects of works of art.

One function of criticism, however, lies in a range between the analytic and the synthetic; the study of the style of individual artists. Artists develop distinctive conventions or traits that can be detected in anything they do, even through radical shifts of technique and structure. The individual conventions make it possible for us to recognize the author of a work of art because they evoke an image of other works we have seen by the same person; in much the same way we recognize the handwriting or the footstep of an acquaintance. These conventions are distinctive enough to aid us in attributing anonymous works to artists whose style is familiar, and even in selecting from a body of anonymous works those that were done by the same unknown hand. Judgments of this kind are the foundation for further art historical and critical activity, particularly in the study of styles such as those of the past four hundred years, in which individuality is prized. By analytic method, we may categorize all the traits of an artist that appear significant to us, and apply the categories to questionable works.

But, while the analysis of individual traits is easily objectified and apparently "scientific," it is not of itself reliable; if it were, copies and forgeries would never pass for originals (indeed, copyists and forgers often assemble in one work more of a master's characteristic conventions than we can find in any authentic product). This is because the sense of individual style also is based on the peculiar over-all tone or quality that can be found in anything a particular artist does; the relative role of quantitative evidence and intuitive "feel," by which we apprehend the quality of the whole, are as indeterminate in our judgment of artistic individuality as in our judgment of the people we meet.

An individual style is like a personality; in defining it we do not necessarily make judgments of value; bad habits are as revealing as good ones; great artists have off-days, and supposedly inferior ones can perform brilliantly. If judgments of this kind are to be trustworthy, they must be based upon a body of knowledge and experience first, of the individual artistic personality and second of the degree to which that personality may be differentiated from others like it. But knowledge and experience may be of no avail; in the study of art as in life there are good and poor, honest and dishonest judges of character, and the latter may be even more learned and experienced than the former. The judgment of personality is a factor of the judge's personality, and it cannot be made empirical. What makes it possible to proceed further on the basis of attributions reached in such an "unscientific" way is the fact that the wrong conclusion can be rejected rather easily even when we are not equipped to improve upon it, and the right one may be confirmed slowly by virtue of having survived a succession of challenges. It is like hiring a man on the recommendation of a personnel expert; if he is poorly equipped for the job we soon discover it, though we may be unable to recommend a better candidate; but if he is fully qualified, the proof emerges only gradually as he is confronted by a variety of new problems.

I have suggested that the idiosyncratic traits of an artist are not necessarily marks of quality; they serve to individualize good and bad art alike, and may be found in fashion drawings as well as in masterpieces. Yet individual habits may be a factor in our enjoyment of a work of art; we may like those of a given artist as we like, say, a certain violinist or conductor, more or less independently of the works in which we see or hear them displayed. Western criticism has put a high premium on individuality, with the result that idiosyncracies may be not simply accepted but actually sought. The premium placed on the casual and revealing gesture in recent abstract art has been pursued on such a scale that a would-be mark of individuality paradoxically has become a convention. In products of cultures more tightly organized than ours, the individual trait is absorbed into the group trait, but the difference is not significant for criticism. Chinese bronzes and Egyptian statues reveal a definable personality, but it is more collective than individual.

In sum, while the traits of artistic personality, like conventions, may be represented analytically, we cannot construct an image of the way they are integrated in an artist's work—as the historian must in solving problems of authorship—without a sense of the total personality, the spirit as well as the "hand." This brings us further into the range of intuitive criticism.

As we proceed from studying the physical character of the work of art to the traits of personality revealed by the artist, we pass from aspects that are the least individualized to those that are the most. Objects of comparable size and material are found in many cultures; certain symbols or modes of composition are found in many works but within only one culture; while a particular handling of line and color may be found in the art of only one person. The final stage in the critical process is the exposition of the uniqueness of the single work of art. This uniqueness already is implied in a negative sense in empirical and analytic observations, which equip us to say that a certain material, technique, or symbol is *not* found in other works by the same artist or in the same culture. But if we want to represent it in a positive sense, we no longer can objectify our statements by proving them against conventional standards of measurement or by comparing two or more works of art. So the process of articulating the uniqueness of the individual work generally is called subjective or intuitive. I call it synthetic, since it no longer defines a trait or component of the work, but its total import for the observer.

As a student I was warned that statements that cannot be readily objectified or proved by techniques of comparison are "unsound." Perhaps good advice for students, but maturer scholars might measure it against a proposition of information theory, that the most easily communicable message conveys less information than the more complex and individualized one. So we value most highly the work of art or of criticism that stimulates responses in us that expand our realm of experience beyond its customary limits. We therefore think of the superior work of art as one that "rises above" its material, technical, and conventional exigencies, and of the superior critic as one who is able to crown his empirical and analytic exposition with revealing syntheses. The difficulty of such synthetic criticism is that it must employ conventional language—as the artist employs his conventional tools—to surpass the limits of convention. Words in their normal functions carry us only to the border of artistic creativity; to penetrate beyond is itself a creative act.

Ordinarily criticism is content to describe effects but not causes of the experience of works of art. For example, Chartres Cathedral is "uplifting," a Rembrandt portrait has a "profound humanity." But what is being described is largely the reaction to conventions. *All* Gothic cathedrals could be called uplifting, and *all* competent Baroque portraits of sad old men, humane. The issue for the critic is why and how Chartres and the Rembrandt portrait are more so. No inventory of separate elements will answer that question, for anything that can be detached from its context can become a convention that a follower could emulate. It is a question of the import of the whole. The work of art is a product of the artistic personality at a given moment; to judge it in terms of its parts would be equivalent to judging a person's expression of feeling by his gesture or his facial configuration or his words or their tone but not by the entire effect. At this point we may abandon the simile of artistic and human personality, for they communicate in different ways. It is not necessary to be a good man in order to make a good statue, or to be a Christian in order to design Chartres; Rembrandt was not known to be a good judge of character. Great art is the transfiguration of commonplace experience by a vision that belongs to art and not by love, faith, philosophy, or other virtues or accomplishments of personality in the usual sense.

To convey the uniqueness of a work of art the critic requires first a sensitivity to and understanding of the work and second the creative capacity to turn his visual experience into verbal discourse. What he describes is the experience of his encounter with the work; but if his description contains too much of his own contribution to the encounter, what he says will be meaningful only to him and will not enlighten his readers. Conversely, if he submerges himself with the intention of "letting the work speak for itself" his intervention becomes superfluous; the work might as well speak directly to the reader. The first of these flaws was attributed to the typical critic at the start of this chapter, and the second to the typical historian.

The historian who wants to avoid the problem of synthesis restricts his attention to physical description and to the analysis of conventions. In recent times, the study of conventions has been fragmented into specialties: formal analysis, iconography (the study of symbolic conventions) and connoisseurship (the study of individual traits). This restriction is adequate for tracing the history and evolution of style, because it operates with the extrinsic characteristics of works of art. But it implies a renunciation of the attempt to discover and reveal in a single work of art anything but the traits it shares with other works or with other aspects of the culture that produced it, so that its individuality can be defined only on negative grounds, and its significance can be measured only mechanically in terms of its influence in establishing new conventions.

By comparing the single work to others in the same milieu, we can make a quantitative account of the extent to which it is distinguishable from others that observe like conventions. But a qualitative account is important for historical as well as critical activity—not the number of unique traits, or the degree of uniqueness of any one, but the impact of the whole that can be experienced but that cannot be tabulated. This force is the only basis for distinguishing mere innovations or idiosyncracy from substantial artistic achievement.

I cannot define the nature of this experience in the abstract because it is the outcome of an encounter of a particular observer and a particular work of art in which both contribute to an aesthetic event. If the observer's understanding of the work is a function of his knowledge, his habits of perception and sensitivity, then there is no meaning in questions such as "What is the aesthetic experience?" Maybe this is why the literature of aesthetics over the centuries has failed to agree upon even the most fundamental rules for answering questions of this kind.

Still, without defining what art is, we realize that we get from it something different than from other forms of communication. We do learn how men of greater genius and sensitivity than ourselves visualize reality, but we gain something beyond information and intellectual enrichment, which we speak of as emotional or spiritual. In this, our relationship to art resembles our relationship to people, in that it may be intimate, shocking, or passionate; but more than most human relationships, it also generates reactions rooted in our physical form and functions. Our responses to symmetry, rhythm, scale, for example, are keyed to the structure of the body and the beat of the heart. So, unlike any other products of the imagination (e.g., in philosophy, science, law) art is a medium for the communication of human feeling. Because there is a consistency to human feelings and physical structure throughout all time and irrespective of cultural differences, this peculiar province of art is by no means inaccessible to critical communication.

If, as I have suggested, the entire range of criticism involves the objectification of subjective reponses, then the attempt to articulate judgments of quality or value cannot be evaded as especially ephemeral or unreliable. These judgments are integral factors in our responses; we may form them more distinctly than other responses. They are not, then, in a distinct realm of experience. Indeed, value distinctions cannot be avoided even by the most "scientific" historians. The decision that one theme is more promising than another in initiating new research, the selection of one work rather than another to illustrate the achievement of an age or of an artist, are based on such distinctions.

This is not to say that every judgment is equally valid. We call some responsible, by which we mean that the critic clearly articulates the grounds on which they are made and demonstrates persuasively how his conclusions may be justified within his terms. Others, which we call irresponsible, are merely the assertion of private responses reflecting mere bias or the unconscious inheritance of the principles of someone else. So the danger of misleading evaluation is paradoxically the greatest in those who believe they are not judging at all.

Suspicion among scholars of the problems of evaluation comes from a justified mistrust of shifting standards of taste. But the issue of taste need not enter. Our taste is a response to materials, techniques, or conventions exclusive of their embodiment in works of art. Since it is not stimulated by specific works, it resides entirely within us, and whether it makes a specific work more or less pleasing to us, it may not help us to see it or, if we are engaged in criticism, to suggest its unique nature. What matters in communicating our judgments is not whether we like or dislike a work of art but whether we do or do not find in it a synthesis that surpasses convention.

While historians and critics alike benefit from considering the entire range of the spectrum of criticism, there are aspects of each vocation that justify the distinction we make between them. History is more concerned with the reconstruction of the context in which works of art are produced; criticism more with the articulation of responses to works of art in relation to current modes of thought. But the difference is one of degree rather than of kind; criticism takes the lead in the study of contemporary art because the special tools of history are difficult to use profitably amid the profusion of data. Where data are sparse, as in the study of extinct civilizations, effective criticism is impossible without substantial historical preparation (e.g., the evaluation of a primitive or prehistoric work without knowledge of the function it served, the meaning of its symbolic conventions, or the distinction between the conventions of the group and those of the individual artist). So, where historical data are profuse, criticism takes the initiative, aiding the historian to distinguish relevant from irrelevant data (critical judgments have prompted historians to document extensively the art of Picasso and Le Corbusier, while thousands of "lesser" contemporaries, even successful ones, go unrecorded); where they are sparse, archaeology and history take the initiative, uncovering sufficient information on the context of works of art to support responsible criticism. In practice, the contrast is more extreme: between journalistic criticism as the arbiter of taste and the empirical research of archivists, editors of sources, catalogers, etc. But the extremes are not equivalent; the former is an ephemeral luxury, while the latter is the essential foundation of the historical disciplines.

Somewhere between, criticism and history merge in a superior alloy; its composition cannot be quite constant, for every critic-scholar must mix it according to his own recipe. Some will lean more toward conveying the individuality of works of art, others more toward the problems of culture or style. The former may select the art that they are able to experience most fully, while the latter may penetrate unexplored reaches to discover even in strange and uncongenial art fresh facets of the human imagination. But, however composed, the alloy is stronger than its component metals.

3

STYLE

Art historians are especially preoccupied with defining the nature and behavior of style.[1] For history to be written at all we
must find in what we study factors that at once are consistent
enough to be distinguishable and changeable enough to have a
"story." In political-social history these factors are sometimes
institutions, sometimes persons or groups—units that retain
their identity over a span of time or shift of locale, yet change
and develop as they react to their environment and its changes.

In the study of the arts, works—not institutions or people—
are the primary data; in them we must find certain characteristics that are more or less stable, in the sense that they appear
in other products of the same artist(s), era or locale, and flexible, in the sense that they change according to a definable
pattern when observed in instances chosen from sufficiently extensive spans of time or of geographical distance. A distinguishable ensemble of such characteristics we call a style.

We use the concept of style, then, as a way of characterizing
relationships among works of art that were made at the same
time and/or place, or by the same person or group. If we do
not know where, when, or by whom works of art were produced,
then the process may be inverted to allow hypotheses that
works of the same style are from the same time, place, or per-
son(s). In this second role, style is an indispensable historical

[1] Since this chapter appeared as "A Theory of Style" in the *Journal of
Aesthetics and Art Criticism,* XX (1962), 227-37, I have taken the opportunity to make some changes prompted by the cordial and penetrating criticisms of Herbert Blau, Donald Egbert, Walter Hipple, Timothy
Kitao, Thomas Parkinson, and Leo Steinberg.

tool; it is more essential to the history of art than to any other historical discipline.

Because works of art are preserved for reasons other than their historical or biographical significance, they often lose all extrinsic evidence of their historical position, so that no record survives of the artist(s), era, or locale that produced them. Without such evidence—coordinates of time and space—it is impossible to plot the graphs of consistency and change that are a prerequisite for the writing of history. But isolated fragments of evidence may be extended into a credible historic account by conclusions based on style; one signed work may be sufficient to construct the whole production of an artist, one dated work to associate a type of art with an epoch.

Style thus provides a structure for the history of art. Other structures are possible (e.g., the biography of artists), but that of style is the most comprehensive, since it is the only one that can be built with minimal external documentation on the evidence of works of art alone. Because our image of style is not discovered but created by abstracting certain features from works of art for the purpose of assisting historical and critical activity, it is meaningless to ask, as we usually do, "What is style?" The relevant question is rather "What definition of style provides the most useful structure for the history of art?"

I suggested that the concept of style is a means of establishing *relationships* among individual works of art. In this it resembles the concepts of society and culture, which are based on similar definitions of relationships; anthropologists also use the word *style* to designate a complex of behavior patterns within a society. There is no objective correlative for our image of a style; we may observe and define certain traits or characteristics in a single work of art, but we cannot call them traits of Rembrant's style, Gothic style, or Tuscan style without summoning our experience of other works by Rembrandt, or the "Gothic period" (which is itself a historian's invention), or from Tuscany. A particular work of art therefore may represent or exemplify characteristics of a style in the way that a person may represent a society, but to say that it has a style, as we often do, is not illuminating. The word *style* defines a certain currency—distinguishable in the work (or in some portion of the work) of an artist, a place, or a time—and it is inefficient to use it also to define the unique traits of single works of art; uniqueness and currency are incompatible. The virtue of the concept of style is that by defining *relationships* it makes various kinds of order out of what otherwise would be a vast continuum of self-sufficient products.

In using an image of style to establish orderly relationships among works of art, we follow the path of the artist, who—by accepting or altering certain features of the arts around him—establishes a relationship that is the predominant factor in the formation of his individual style. For the artist and for his audience, style is a protection against chaos; it serves the same purpose as do cultural patterns and institutions in society. A class of works of art of any kind—pyramids, portraits of rulers, still lifes—is orderly and distinguishable because it is necessary to human beings not only to express themselves within established patterns, but to experience the world around them in accordance with such patterns; our perceptual mechanisms cause us to interpret what we see in terms of what we know and expect. The factor of stability in style can be traced to a sort of inertia; presumably, if natural inclinations were undisturbed by imagination, ambition and other desires, society and language would remain fixed and art would have a history of more or less competent copies of the work of some Daedalic demigod. But we are mercifully favored with passions that struggle with—though they never quite overcome—that inertia, and these contribute the flexible factor in style.

The artist submits to this tension between stability and change, between the reproduction of existing forms and the invention of new ones, by necessity, not by choice. Unlike a machine, he cannot reproduce without inventing, for when change is not prompted by inventiveness it is prompted by boredom. So art has never been static; when it is not vital, it actively degenerates. Conversely, the artist cannot invent without reproducing; in order to make a meaningful innovation he must be able to concentrate his forces upon the few aspects of his work where circumstances favor fresh departures; for the rest, he relies on the support of his tradition and of his environment. An artist cannot invent himself out of his time and, if he could, he would succeed only in making his work incomprehensible by abandoning the framework in which it might be understood.

The relationship of stability and change varies according to the pace and degree of individualization of a culture; in recent art a powerful factor of flexibility causes radical shifts of style in the course of a generation, while in ancient Egypt stability predominated to the point that barely perceptible innovations were sufficient to secure the vitality of a style for three millennia.

In the tradition of modern Western criticism, the forces that make for change in art have been praised more warmly than those that make for stability. Since the Romantic period the military hero has been admired more for his adventurousness than for his caution, and the artist-hero more for his innovations than for his ability to sustain tradition. This preference exemplifies a "progressive" view of art opposed, presumably, to a conservative view that would favor the forces of stability. Neither is really relevant to criticism. Change and stability simply are primeval forces in style and cannot be invested with value except in terms of some preconceived image of man's destiny.

If the characteristics of the work of art that contribute to a definition of style must exhibit some stability and flexibility, then all of its possible characteristics cannot contribute in equal measure. Conventions of form and of symbolism yield the richest harvest of traits by which to distinguish style. I mean by conventions an accepted vocabulary of elements—a scale of color, an architectural order, an attribute of a god or a saint— and a syntax by which these elements are composed into a still life, a temple, or a frieze. We get an image of the style of an individual by observing the interaction of his private conventions and the public conventions of his time and place. Since conventions, like language, are the basic vehicle for the communication of meaning, society aids the artist in promoting their stability and in controlling the rate, the degree, and even the nature of their change. Religious symbolism, for example, is determined by religious establishments as well as by artists, and other less utilitarian conventions, such as those of landscape painting or of recent abstract art, are sustained, if not formulated, by the needs of an economically powerful class.

Other inherent characteristics help less in determining style; aspects of the work of art as a material object change so little in the course of history that they might appear almost anywhere at any time. So to say that a painting is done on wood, that a statue weighs three hundred pounds, or that a building is thirty feet high is to make a statement that, for all its precision, conveys little of style.

Technique, or the process by which matter is given form, is a more sensitive gauge of style than the strictly material aspect of the work of art, but less sensitive than the conventional character. To say that a temple is constructed of doweled ashlar blocks and that its trussed roof rests on lintels supported by columns is to reveal more of its style than to say that it is built of marble, wood, and iron; but it does not distinguish a Greek temple from a Roman or Neoclassic one.

Yet technique may be a fundamental stylistic determinant; this occurs because usually it is not merely a means, but serves important formal or symbolic functions. In Gothic architecture the ribbed vault, which represents a substantial advance in engineering, is not just a device for achieving an expressive form; it is itself an expressive form, whereas in the skyscraper design of the last generation, the aim to "reveal" the skeletal steel frame in the exterior design had a symbolic motivation. (The skeleton, in fact, had to be covered for fire protection; its reflection in the façade design, often achieved artificially, symbolized "honesty.") Gothic and early twentieth century architects were uncommonly interested in structure, and their interest promoted an extraordinary flexibility in technique. Structural change in Gothic architecture was so rapid and so rational that it can be traced systematically in a succession of cathedrals started within the same generation; vaulting or buttressing methods alone are sufficient to provide a key to chronology. By contrast, the technical change in other great phases of European architecture—from 550 to 350 B.C. or from A.D. 1450 to 1650 —was negligible, almost an insignificant component of style.

One of the most stubborn and challenging problems of art history is to explain the motivations and behavior of change in style. While this involves concentration on flexible factors, we could not separate one style from another, or speak of a style, without first defining it in terms of stable factors. We create classes such as Impressionism, Baroque art, or Picasso's Blue Period on the assumption that a certain complex of elements common to a group of works is sufficiently stable, distinct, and relevant to justify characterizing it as a style. In a similar way, political historians distinguish "periods" within the constant flux of human action—the Middle Ages, the Reformation, or the Colonial Era—in terms of what they believe to be cohesive and significant social events. This definition of a style in terms of its stable factors is a hypothesis (and one that we must challenge constantly) that makes it possible to study change.

While style usually can be defined in reference to a more or less fixed block of historical time, the study of its processes of change requires reference to the succession of events within that block.

For most of the five hundred years of modern art history the patterns of change have been described in biological metaphors. Vasari, the most scholarly historian of the Renaissance, believed that style, "like human bodies, has a birth, a growth, an aging and a death." The scheme survived into the last century, when it got refinements from Darwin and his colleagues and when terms such as *the evolution* (or *life*) *of style* entered our vocabulary.² Most of Vasari's followers before 1850 were interested chiefly in the art of two epochs—antiquity and the Renaissance —which were susceptible to being fit into the biological life cycle, and even those who turned from Classicism toward the Gothic found that the formula still could be used. Toward the end of the last century, scientific scholarship and the broadening of taste encouraged a more specific and less normative model of evolution from an archaic to a classic to a baroque phase. There remained, however, a bias in favor of the classic; the Parthenon, Amiens, and Raphael were thought to be peaks of the cycle (as expressed in the terms *High Gothic; High Renaissance*) toward which earlier artists aspired and from which later artists retreated.

At the turn of the century, Alois Riegl, who supported his theory of style with studies of nonclassical phases (late Roman, early Baroque art), was influential in persuading colleagues to grant equality to all phases. He promoted a principle that typifies art history in this century, that the best solution to an artistic

² Historians of the last century who adopted evolutionary metaphors generally misapplied them in support of deterministic theories of history (aided by some evolutionists who also were teleologists and "vitalists"). But modern evolutionary theory discourages all such efforts, and indeed offers the most convincing support for the nondeterminist kind of interpretation I am proposing here. See, e.g., George G. Simpson, *The Meaning of Evolution* (Yale, 1949, 1960).

problem is the one that best fulfills the artist's aim. But this relativism in the sphere of value was accompanied by determinism in explaining the dynamics of style; in place of the biological metaphor, Riegl put cycles of evolution from an early "haptic" to a later "optic" phase. At the same time, Heinrich Wölfflin offered a still more influential theory of preordained evolution from classical to baroque form in terms of polar formal categories: closed-open, linear-painterly, etc. As compared to the biological tradition, which had the disadvantage of being applicable to only three of the major styles of Western art, that of Riegl and Wölfflin describes more universal patterns of style, though eras remain—among them Carolingian and nineteenth century art—that give little support to their systems. In the past half century no new theories of style have taken root; in this country none were even proposed until quite recently.[3] This is not due so much to satisfaction with earlier theories as to the rise of a narrow scientism that has made philosophical speculation suspect. Although we cannot work without a theory of style, and although we continue to speak of classical, baroque, or painterly forms, we have allowed the systems that give meaning to these terms to slip into the unconscious, where they operate without the benefit of our control, as a barrier against new perceptions.

All of the major theories of style have been determinist in the sense that they define a preordained pattern of "evolution": the earlier phase of a style is *destined* to move toward the later. This is to say that at any stage in the process some force other than the will of artists must be at work directing invention toward the goal that ultimately is to be achieved. Twentieth cen-

[3] See Vincent Scully, "The Nature of the Classical in Art," *Yale French Studies,* XIX/XX (1957), 107 ff.; J. S. Ackerman, "Art History and the Problems of Criticism," *Daedalus* (Winter 1960), pp. 253 ff. (reprinted in *The Visual Arts Today,* ed. Gyorgy Kepes [Wesleyan U.P., 1960]); Lincoln Rothschild, *Style in Art* (Yoseloff, 1960); and George Kubler, *The Shape of Time* (Yale, 1962).

tury scholars do not grant a priority of value to any phase of the evolution, but a value concept lurks in the shadows; if it is the destiny of styles to evolve as they did, then those works of art that promoted that evolution are destiny-fulfilling and those that did not are destiny-denying. The implication that the former are superior cannot be avoided. So, in our handbooks of the history of styles it appears that the chief function of any work of art is to contribute toward the works that follow it in a sequence; and the greater the contribution the more "significant" the work. The history of art has been fashioned into another version of the materialist success story.[4]

It is easy to understand how historians studying Greek, Gothic, or Renaissance art first formulated a biological model and later a more sophisticated theory of an innate dynamics of style; in those periods the sequence of works is so evident, the number of "unsuccessful" productions so few, that it appears almost inevitable that the Temple of Hera at Olympia should have led ultimately to the Parthenon, or the portal sculpture of the façade of Chartres to that of Rheims and finally to that by Claude Sluter. The process is orderly; it is similar in ancient Greece and late medieval Europe, which otherwise are dissimilar civilizations, and finally it is so much like biological growth that we are tempted almost irresistibly to define it as natural or necessary. At the least it would seem that the designer of Olympia and the sculptors of Chartres were making the first steps toward the goal that was gained by their successors.

But the account of a sequence of increasingly successful solutions to a problem contains a concealed germ of determinism.

[4] See Meyer Schapiro's classic survey and critique of style theory in *Anthropology Today,* ed. A. L. Kroeber (U. of Chicago, 1953), pp. 287-312; reprinted in *Aesthetics Today,* ed. Morris Philipson (Meridian, 1961), pp. 81-113. My earlier statement on this subject, "Art History and the Problems of Criticism" (see note 3), was criticized by Thomas Munro in the *Journal of Aesthetics and Art Criticism,* XIX (1961), 414 f.

It introduces a trap into which historians habitually fall, as a result of the benefits of hindsight. When we review the surviving evidence of a process in the past we can see the effects as well as the causes of any event within the process. We can, for example, designate a work from a later moment as a "classic" solution and judge any earlier work according to what it contributed or failed to contribute to that solution. Or, with Wölfflin, we can praise—or cite as especially significant—solutions in the classic phase that contributed most to the making of the baroque phase.

We cannot erase our image of the totality of a style process in the past, but this need not discourage us from trying to interpret a work of art in terms of its proper context rather than its effects by gaining perspectives *within* the process at points short of its termination. At any one of these points we shall find an artist making a statue or designing a cathedral. He, too, is aware of works preceding his, and of works being made by his contemporaries, and these constitute an important source in the formation of his style. Given our habits of hindsight, it is necessary to add that he is not aware of the works that will follow his; he knows only past and present. He accepts and rejects aspects of what he finds in things about him and he adds something of his own. By his choice and by his contribution he moves a step—sometimes a leap—away from the past. Are we, then, justified in saying that he has moved toward the future?

In his terms the future is a void—how can he move toward it? If he dreams of its wonders, the dreams themselves, like his art, are creations of the present. He may happen to contribute to the future, but only by having concentrated primarily on the making of something intrinsically worthwhile in the present. If the sculptors at Chartres had visualized as the ultimate goal of their effort something like the Rheims figures, they surely would have carved something like the Rheims figures. Anyone who seeks to alter or to accelerate the change of style primarily in the hope of anticipating the future is likely to become, like the fashion designer, an expert in and purveyor of taste.[5]

What ultimately prevents an artist from controlling the future is the unpredictable behavior of his successors. His effect upon them is partly a matter of chance. It depends on his work being seen by someone and, if it is, on the receptivity of those who see it. Powerfully expressive works are more likely to be influential than weaker ones, but often they are rejected vigorously even by artists—not only when they are considered too radical (Michelangelo's late pietàs; William Blake's paintings) but even when they are considered not radical enough (Botticelli in 1505, Ingres in 1860).

These observations suggest a different approach to defining the process of change in style. What is called evolution in the arts should not be described as a succession of steps toward a solution to a given problem, but as a succession of steps away from one or more original statements of a problem. Each step, for the artist who takes it, is a probe that reaches to the limits of his imagination; he cannot consciously make a transition to a succeeding step, for if he visualizes something he regards as preferable to what he is doing, he presumably will proceed to do it, unless he is constrained in some way. So we cannot speak

---

[5] I received some warranted criticism of my initial phrasing of this idea (article cited in note 3), which suggested that artists are not prophets, that they communicate present experience, not hope for the future. I should have seen that artists, like most of the rest of us, are eager to leave an imprint on the future, and that, unlike many of us, they may, if they are gifted and win an audience, be effective prophets. Many works of art, particularly since the Renaissance, have been motivated in part by the artist's desire to change the world. In my eagerness to attack historical determinism I failed to point out that while the ability of a particular work of art to compel a following is not *necessarily* a sign of its greatness, it can be. Thus historians and critics are justified in pointing to the impact of masterpieces on future generations as material evidence of their stature, so long as they do not invert the argument to use the quantity of influence of a given work as a measure of its quality.

properly of a sequence of solutions to a given problem, since with each solution the nature of the problem changes.

We might visualize a style as a great canvas on which generations of artists have painted. The earliest ones set out a composition; later ones keep some of it, rub some out, and add some of their own; the next do the same and so on. At any moment in the process there is a complete picture, but no indication of what it will look like after the succeeding artist has done his share. At the close of the process, when some artists have started on another picture, this one is abandoned. But the final image, although composed of contributions from every artist, cannot be said to represent the aims of the earlier ones, or to represent a solution to the problem posed by the first of them.

The pattern of style change, then, is not determined by any destiny or by a common goal, but by a succession of complex decisions as numerous as the works by which we have defined the style. We can detect a pattern or distinguish a common problem because each decision in turn, by its choice of elements that are to be retained or rejected, and by its innovations, gives to the whole a determinable configuration. The configuration may *appear* purposeful or predestined because each successive work retains something of those that precede it and because its innovations, though not anticipated in earlier works, are coherently related to them. But what actually motivates the process is a constant incidence of probings into the unknown, not a sequence of steps toward the perfect solution.

So we return to an earlier observation that the pattern of change is a product of the tension in society and in the artist between the instinct for the stability and security of established schemes and the human capacity (resulting partly from biological and psychological differences) for creating something unique and individualized. Change is slow when the former is stronger, rapid when the latter prevails. As a rule, the factor of stability gets more support from society and its institutions, and the factor of change from the individual imagination; creative vision seldom is granted to groups. On the rare occasion when inspired patronage (Emperor Frederick II, Louis XIV) does more than the artist to motivate a style, the patron proves to be a creative individual who deserves to be called an artist. Given our background in the dialectic of German art history, it is necessary to emphasize that a nation, a religion, a *Zeitgeist,* is likely, except in its formative stage, to *resist rather than to promote* change in style. The idea that Germans, Roman Catholics, or Baroque Man embody a creative expressive will (I am recalling Riegl's "Kunstwollen") apart from the contributions of their artists I find incomprehensible and distasteful. If German art is German, it is not because any creative innovation in it has been produced by a mystical German Spirit, but because the nation and its artists show a tendency to keep certain kinds of innovation and to cast out other kinds. It is by this conservative, post facto, pressure that society affects art.

In proposing an alternative to current interpretations of patterns of change in style, I do not want to overrate the significance of chronological succession. To do so is to imply that each work necessarily is related more closely to its immediate predecessors than to others of an earlier stage of a style or in what we have defined as different styles. Indeed, the demands of society and the inclinations of artists make the innovations of the latest work by contemporaries in the same culture especially interesting, because they represent attempts to solve in a familiar language the kind of problem that is challenging at the moment. But the creative process is complex enough to be stimulated at many points; often the art of earlier times or of foreign places offers solutions to such problems, too—it even may suggest new problems, since its language is less familiar. So inspiration may come from far as well as from near; sometimes, especially in the formulation of a new problem, the distant past is actually closer than yesterday, as Roman art was closer than

Gothic to the early Renaissance or primitive sculpture closer than Impressionism to some painters of the early 1900's.

In visualizing a style process, then, we must keep in mind that the individual innovations that give it pattern may be motivated as easily from outside as from within the style itself. Since the artist may experience and put to use in making a work of art anything in his environment, the historian must reconstruct as much of that environment as possible. Each work of art can be considered a repository of experiences entering from every direction in the artist's surroundings. That it owes a special debt to great predecessors in the same tradition, to the artist's teachers and colleagues, is no more than a plausible hypothesis; the role of these likely contributors must be weighed against that of all the works of art and other possible visual and nonvisual stimuli available to the artist.

This contextual approach—establishing an open, as opposed to a closed, system—has been used by the best modern historians and need not be described in detail, but the absence of it in a majority of studies, particularly those devoted to the work of individual artists, causes the assumption of an internal "evolution" from one work to the next to gain precedence over a deep analysis of the genesis of each work in succession.

My primary aim is to explain change in style as the manifestation rather of the imagination of individual artists than of historical forces that guide the actions of men and nations. But if we attributed every aspect of change to the operation of individual free will, we should not be able to explain the crucial phenomenon that originally encouraged deterministic and evolutionary theories: that sequences in quite different cultures may reveal similar patterns of change. In Greek, Gothic, and Renaissance art there appears to be a phase of equilibrium (usually described as *classic*) preceded by a more formalized, and followed by a freer phase. The fact that this pattern cannot be found in every sequence (e.g., Roman, Carolingian, nine-teenth century art) does not lessen our responsibility to explain it where it can be found, if it really is, as I believe, justified by the evidence of the monuments themselves. The problem is to discover an explanation of recurrent patterns that avoid on the one hand the tyranny of external historical forces or laws, and on the other hand the anarchy of mere chance.

Perhaps the clearest instance of a recurrent pattern in art is in the development of techniques from a stage of crudity and exploration to a stage of refinement. Sculptors, for example, may learn to carve with greater finesse or to cast more and more complex forms up to a point at which they attain—within the requirements of their style—a maximal potential for their body, tools, and materials. But technique does not always behave in this way; desire for progress in finesse occurs with variable intensity and even may be absent. Nor is it always possible, for some problems are solved at the start of a style, as when the Van Eycks, the first great painters to adopt oil glazes, achieved in their earliest surviving pictures a technical perfection that was never surpassed and rarely equalled.

There is no predetermined law of technical progress any more than there is a law of stylistic evolution. Even where we find techniques systematically refined to a point at which they reach their maximal potential, the succeeding steps cannot be predicted; at that point, artists may abandon the benefits of finesse (Manet as against the Salon painters); maintain the level achieved (Renaissance sculpture after Donatello) or be unable to sustain a high level of performance (mosaics and stained glass after 1300).

But while technique need not progress in refinement, it often does progress, and where technical problems are similar in different styles, the pattern of the progress is similar. Figural stone sculpture in the round is found in many diverse cultures; the typical pattern of change begins with stiff, frontal, and blocky figures and passes on to more mobile and rounded ones. One reason for this is that the technique of carving stone with a metal instrument does not change fundamentally; in any epoch the beginner has difficulty in turning a block into a human figure without retaining a blocklike character. The stone and the chisel impose their own laws that the artist must obey, and this is true at the most refined as well as at the most primitive level; there is a limit to freedom, to the length an unsupported arm can be extended without breaking, to the amount that can be cut from the lower position of the block without weakening the superstructure. Such limits—together with the classical heritage—explain certain similarities between highly developed techniques in different eras (the figure in Hellenistic sculpture, Bernini, Canova).

We find another example of the pressures exerted on the artist by technique in the development of skeletal structure in Gothic architecture. The invention of the rib vault and the flying buttress made it possible to lighten vaults and walls, which had been uniformly massive in Romanesque building, by concentrating stresses in chosen points. The lightening process was barely noticeable in the first experiments with bulky members, but once conceived, it was continued to the limit of the structural strength of stone (and even beyond, as demonstrated by the collapse of the choir of Beauvais Cathedral). A similar development of skeletal structures occurred with the introduction of the steel frame in the last century, in that it encouraged a systematic development away from massiveness and a metamorphosis of the masonry wall into glass, as in Gothic architecture.

In discussing figural sculpture and skeletal structure I have implied that there is something about the posing of the technical problem that suggests the direction in which a succession of solutions is likely to move. But what that something is cannot be explained in terms of technique alone; it is also a matter of formal and symbolic aims. What impels an artist along the path toward finesse is not so much a love of skill for its own sake as the conception of forms that are beyond the reach of existing skills. In figural sculpture this conception often has something to do with imitation; the style is drawn from its blocky beginnings to freer and more rounded forms because the human body is freer and more rounded than a block. So long as each artist in turn is intrigued by the problem of mimesis the process is likely to continue along the scale from the blocky to the illusionistic. The aims seldom are so simple; in one sense archaic Greek figural sculptors followed such a path, but at the same time they became increasingly intrigued by a sophisticated linear refinement that was not illusionistic; sculptors of the early fifth century B.C. had to reject that refinement vigorously in order to resume the mimetic process; but they in turn were drawn to idealization and generalization as well as to imitation of the human body.

The appeal of illusion best illustrates how the acceptance of a problem directs the artist, for he continually may adjust his art to conform to his perceptions of the world about him. The notebooks of Leonardo da Vinci are evidence of just this process of adjustment; nature is taken to be an objective goal toward which art can and should strive, and minute observations of it are systematically translated into the terms of painting. But the example of Gothic architecture proves how problems that cannot be solved by models in nature may still guide the process of solutions. The development of the skeletal structure was motivated, among other things, by a continuing desire to get more light. So long as this desire prevailed, the revision of forms was bound to be in the direction of substituting glass for stone—first, by concentrating stresses in the skeleton, and second by reducing the mass of the skeleton itself.

These observations do not modify my earlier strictures against predetermined patterns. The artist involved in such a process need not be striving toward a distant and unobtainable goal; he merely may be refining the solution of his predecessor. So the Gothic architect might say "At Soissons they managed to get more glass and thinner piers than at Paris but I shall do still better." He did not have the "classic" solution of Amiens in mind. The same psychology would apply even in cases where it might be said that there is only one correct solution, for example, the geometrical projection of a three-dimensional figure onto a two-dimensional plane in Renaissance painting.

One plausible explanation, then, for patterns of change in style is that where a certain problem posed at the start of a style continues to challenge artists over an extended span of time, and only where it suggests one type of solution rather than another, the process will show progressive refinement toward the preferred type of solution. When similar patterns are exhibited in different cultures, it is likely that the preferred type of solution is in some way similar. Refinement of this kind is neither inevitable nor necessarily desirable. The stability of Egyptian art is due to the fact that the solutions found at an early stage were considered optimal for centuries; by contrast, Roman and nineteenth century art tended to shift often from one problem to another. In short, the psychology of artistic production admits but does not demand systematic and recurrent patterns of change in style.

On what grounds may we establish the limits or extent of a style, and differentiate it from other styles? Sometimes the question is partially answered by social-historical phenomena, as in epochs when a new style is started abruptly to satisfy a new need (early Christian architecture) or terminated by disaster or acculturation (Aztec, Northwest Indian art); or when it is co-extensive with a closed political or geographical unit (ancient Egypt). Most of Western art, however, from Greek antiquity to the present day is a great mega-style within which we attempt to find plausible subdivisions that help to clarify the historical process.

Style is not the only framework within which historical process can be studied in the arts. Classes of works exemplifying a particular technique or a formal or symbolic convention reveal processes that may span several styles (e.g., the history of the dome, of perspective, of landscape painting, of the iconography of the immaculate conception). Another kind of framework is formed by the entire body of work produced within an arbitrarily chosen span of time such as a decade, a century, or a political reign. But limits of this kind, which presume some special significance to mere contemporaneity, are less likely to prompt fresh perceptions than those suggested by criteria of style deduced from works of art themselves. The framework most highly favored by students of Renaissance and modern art —lifework of a single artist—is subject to similar deficiencies. It has the apparent advantage that its limits are inexorably fixed by mortality, and that it normally is coextensive with a consistent personal style that behaves as a minuscule echo of larger styles. But the presumption of consistency in human beings is unwarranted; the life span of an individual can be almost as insensitive a measure of style as any arbitrarily chosen segment of time. One artist or the artists of a century may adhere to a single style or shift from one style to another, and in our time such shifts are more the rule than the exception.

We distinguish one style from another by noting differences in the use of conventions, materials, and techniques. We do this by referring to an image of the norms of a style as a whole—style in the stable sense; but the image does not help to determine chronological or geographical limits. We can easily define generic differences between a Gothic and a Renaissance statue without being able to specify which statues are the first works of Renaissance sculpture.

We cannot find a specific moment at which one style gives

way to another because the creative process involved in contributing to the formation of a new style is not of a different order from other creative acts. Both radical and conservative artists choose what they want to retain and what they want to reject from their tradition and contribute something of their own. When the balance favors retention, styles survive; when it favors rejection, they dissipate—though they may flourish, particularly in the provinces, long after desertion by the adherents of a new current. Since the extinction of one style is neither the prerequisite for nor, necessarily, the result of the initiation of another, old and new styles may exist side-by-side and mutually influence one another; and several new ones may coexist even in the same locale. (Paris of the early twentieth century harbored Cubism, Fauvism, Futurism, etc.)

A style, then, may be thought of as a class of related solutions to a problem—or responses to a challenge—that may be said to begin whenever artists begin to pursue a problem or react to a challenge that differs significantly from those posed by the prevailing style or styles. It is easy to detect a "significant" difference when artists vigorously reject major features of a traditional style and consciously aim to eliminate them from their work (Carolingian and Renaissance architecture, most early twentieth century movements); but the distinction is quite unclear when the inventions of an artist who thinks of himself as a faithful bearer of tradition become the nucleus of a wholly new style, and one style flows into another without perceptible deflections. I think of Giotto and Duccio; they represent the flowering of the late Middle Ages and/or the origins of the Renaissance, according to the historian's needs—to his definition of what is significant.

If we accept, then, a theory of confluent, overlapping, and interacting styles in place of a cyclical-evolutionary theory, the problem of fixing limits becomes much less urgent. The cycles of traditional art history must have beginnings and ends and new cycles need to be started by somebody; but the limits of confluent styles such as Gothic-Renaissance or Renaissance-Baroque can be fixed wherever the problem at hand requires, since they admittedly have no objective reality.

So long as it matters a great deal when and by whom a new style is initiated, it is difficult to distinguish the innovator from the genius, for the premium tends to be placed rather on novelty than on quality. While the two are not necessarily antithetical, a theory that exaggerates the importance of the initiation of styles cannot admit a dispassionate examination of the relationship of novelty to quality. The great artist is often an innovator, but his genius does not consist so much in the innovations themselves as in his ability to make them expressive and forceful. Innovations can be made by anyone, and often minor artists have conceived novelties that gained significance and force only in the hands of their betters. It is useful to designate as the start of a style the work of a great master, but often he is only one, and not always the first, to employ the new elements that characterize the style. But by the power of his art he frames the innovations into problems or challenges that continue to absorb his successors for generations. These successors are expressing their respect, not for the novelty but for the quality and authority of certain works of art. Being artists and not chroniclers, they tend to be indifferent to the question of whether those works were the first of their kind.

By taking a neutral position with respect to innovation, we awaken our perceptions to the realm of qualities that distinguished artists evoke from traditional elements in their art. Equally important is the evaluation of "minor" and "unsuccessful" styles, which are forced into the background by cyclical or dialectic theories that allow only one "major development" at one time. Because Leonardo and Raphael were so effective around 1505, the powerful and original art of Botticelli and Piero di Cosimo at the same period has been relegated to obscurity. It is revealing that this art, at the close of the Florentine early Renaissance, should have suffered more from our historical biases than other comparable terminal expressions —the late Michelangelo, El Greco, Vermeer, Turner. I believe that the members of this second group, who had little following in their time (younger artists could not emulate or understand their achievements), were "successful" in modern times because our own art had trained us to appreciate them. A theory that properly accredits the so-called minor and terminal expressions by accentuating the complexity of the context of any work of art should promote a subtler and more penetrating criticism.

If our image of a style is formed about a succession of works that develops the potential of a given problem, then styles of a relatively modest extension make the most rewarding frame for study. Grand, epochal frames such as Renaissance and Baroque are too large to help in making critical distinctions; we cannot agree on defining their problem. Renaissance scholars generally recognize this difficulty, but the monolithic image of the Baroque still causes works of radically opposed styles (Bernini and de Hooch!) to be forced into a single category. At the opposite extreme, the channel of works by a single artist may be too constricted, for reasons that I have already stated.

The subdivision of large epochs into lesser spans (Early and High Renaissance, Mannerism) is a compromise—partly a hangover of the old biological metaphor—which confuses criteria of style (*Mannerism* is a style term) with vague chronological measures (*Early Renaissance* means c. 1400-1500 in Italy and something else in other countries). Categories that are created for the purpose of making distinctions of style should be built logically on criteria of style. Furthermore, since the selection of a style as the object of study inevitably involves a presumption of cohesiveness, it should follow and not precede the hypothesis that a certain group of works is closely integrated and clearly distinguished from other groups. If we assume the existence of a style at the start (a danger with pat concepts such as "classic" and "romantic" periods, etc.) we shall delude ourselves into crowding into it what does not belong.

In this chapter I have tried to define principles based as far as possible on the examination of the creative process, so that the individual work of art, and not the force of some vague destiny, might be seen as the prime mover of the historical process revealed by style. So I have interpreted the concept of a style and of its limits as a generalization that we form, by comparing individual works, into shapes that are convenient for historical and critical purposes. I hope that my image of confluent and concurrent styles, by avoiding the implication of a predetermined evolution and hierarchy of values, may admit a method that is sensitive to the actual causes and effects of works of art, and that it may encourage the interpretation of any creative act in terms of the total context in which it was performed.

4

ART HISTORY IN AMERICA

The development of art history in the United States can be traced in three stages corresponding roughly to three generations; the first was active at the end of the nineteenth century, the second from World War I to 1930, and the third from 1930 to World War II.[1]

The first of these stages was ethical rather than scholarly; the art of the past was studied and taught with little attention to scientific method as a desirable accoutrement of a cultivated person, and almost no one would have thought of doing original research on the works of art. It is curious, in view of the later orientation of the field, that it first assumed a British mould, in the Ruskin tradition; Charles Eliot Norton of Harvard, the father of art history in America, corresponded with Ruskin, Morris, and Carlyle, and was openly scornful of "German erudition," though he was forced to use its products as textbooks. Charles C. Perkins was a lone exception to this rule; a Bostonian who was a patron of the arts (a founder of the Boston Museum of Fine Arts) and a printmaker, he began

---

[1] In view of the number and influence of scholars of European birth and training in American art history, I have arbitrarily designated as American the historian who was a citizen at the completion of his advanced studies.

The theme of this chapter was treated brilliantly a decade ago by Erwin Panofsky's "Three Decades of Art History in the United States" in Franz L. Neumann, et al., The Cultural Migration: The European Scholar in America (U. of Pa., 1953), pp. 82-111; reprinted in Panofsky, Meaning in the Visual Arts (Doubleday [Anchor Books], 1955). For documentation on the first thirty years of the century, see Roberta Fansler and Priscilla Hiss, Research in Fine Arts in the Colleges and Universities of the United States (Carnegie Corp., 1934).

his formal historical training in Leipzig and became the most scholarly American art historian of the century. He published five books on Italian art—mostly sculpture—between 1864 and 1886, the date of his most influential work, *Ghiberti et son école* (could he not find an American publisher?). His example was not followed, probably because he was not at a university.

Although graduate courses were available in the field during the 1890's, the training was more effective in producing gentlemen than scholars, and the majority of able historians of the next generation were raised in other disciplines, particularly in classical archaeology and literature. The archaeologists over-compensated, perhaps, for lack of rigor among the others; they were not so much heirs of Winckelmann and the amateurs of ancient art as of the philological tradition and its excessive emphasis on technique. So an antithesis developed at the very start between the application of critical and historical principles without techniques, and the application of techniques without principles, which ultimately must have encouraged the isolation of criticism from scholarship.

The scholarship of the one outstanding American of the earliest generation, Bernard Berenson, cannot be explained wholly by his background in this country. After studying Near Eastern languages at Harvard, he left the United States for Italy and formed his own kind of art history from reading and meeting Italian and German connoisseurs, historians, and philosophers. Yet there was much of the Norton tradition in Berenson; he was a gentleman to a theatrical degree, though this did not inhibit his painstaking scholarship, and he cultivated British gentlemen-scholars. His early books of the 1890's, addressed like a Harvard course of the time to the interested amateur rather than to fellow scholars, were no longer predominantly ethical, but they vigorously promoted certain aesthetic "values" and presented a brief for Renaissance humanism in the colloquial sense of humaneness. Berenson's fame, although greatly promoted by his personality alone, is a recognition of his stature as the first American of international importance in his field, and one who made a vigorous, if not always successful, attempt to resolve the antithesis between principles and techniques. On the whole, his technique was sounder than his principles, and for this reason, I think that his most lasting contribution may be his catalog of Florentine drawings (*The Drawings of the Florentine Painters,* 3 vols., 1903; rev. ed., 1938, 1961), in which his method and evocative practical criticism are exercised without much involvement in aesthetic or historical theory.

The fact that the science of Berenson and of some of his contemporaries took the form of connoisseurship and the compiling of catalogs (n.b., six volumes, 1912-28, on the sculpture of the della Robbia family by Alan Marquand, founder of the Princeton Department of Art and Archaeology) was related to, if not motivated by the sudden and explosive acceleration of collecting by American tycoons who were new to the art world, were willing to spend millions, and were in need of expert assistance. A few men bought—and are still buying—for America a background in art by creating some of the great museums of the world, and this had an incalculable effect on the growth of art history. From then on, great art was accessible to all Americans rather than to the few who could travel abroad; it was, so to speak, democratized—a process aided by the contemporaneous developments in photographic reproduction that first made it possible to study art at second hand. As this occurred, the ethical-gentlemanly era began to draw to a close in the universities, though it survived, paradoxically, in the museums themselves, as a result of the enforced fealty of curators and directors to wealthy patrons.

Apart from Berenson, whose permanent residence abroad identified him with the stream of European thought, American scholars emerged slowly from provincialism; the universities produced only three doctoral dissertations on fine arts other than classical or American archaeology before World War I, and two were on early Christian archaeology; the first scholarly journal in the field, the *Art Bulletin,* did not appear until 1918, and for several years was padded with inferior contributions on art education and aesthetics. By this time Continental scholarship in the field, which—through the work of such men as Jakob Burckhardt from the 1850's on, Cavalcaselle from the 1860's, Viollet-le-Duc and the French medieval archaeologists—already had gained a respected position among the humanities, was enjoying its golden age; probably a more productive one than any before or since. Maturity for American art history could come only from dependence on the already vast achievement of Europe.

In view of the crisis brought on by the antithesis of the ethical approach and archaeological technique, it is significant that Americans turned for assistance to Continental, especially to German, scholarship at a moment of positivism, when theorizing became suspect and the aim was to establish art history and other humanities as "scientific" disciplines. In the second decade of the twentieth century, the great activity of Berenson's generation in historiography of art and aesthetics (Wölfflin, Riegl, Croce, etc.) lost momentum, as scholars generally began to concentrate more on the refinement of techniques than on principles; it seemed to be sufficient in the course of the next half century to ruminate over—or to attack—definitions of historical change formulated around 1900. The majority of American scholars not only accepted the prevailing antitheoretical mood, but even ignored the existing theories upon which the work of their colleagues abroad had been grounded; the study of historiography was not included in programs of higher education, nor did relevant theoretical activity in neighboring fields—history, anthropology, literature—exercise much influence on art history. So conditions did not favor the formation of distinctive approaches to the field; on the whole, Americans accepted the various European "schools" of art history, not so much by overt choice as by absorption. Still today, because theories of history have not been cultivated consciously, much American scholarship, though dependent on European sources, is inconsistent in applying them and uncertain in the definition of its fundamental concepts.

Discomfort with over-all principles of criticism and history did not prevent the first American experts of 1910-30 from making internationally significant contributions to the field. The second generation was distinguished by an extraordinary perseverence and enthusiasm in the search for unknown monuments and documents, especially when they were to be found in inaccessible places (such as the Pyrenees and other unpaved parts of Spain, which attracted Georgiana Goddard King, Kingsley Porter, Chandler Post, Walter Cook, and others during the 1920's), and by a flair for bold—occasionally reckless —hypotheses (such as Berenson's technique of inventing artists solely on the grounds of groups of related paintings; Kingsley Porter's redating of nearly all Romanesque sculpture; C. R. Morey's vision of a great and influential survival of antique art in Alexandria, of W. M. Ivins in his studies of the role of perception in the arts). Few of them were drawn to familiar fields with rich bibliographies; they did not study Santa Sofia but the desert churches of Syria, not Amiens but the destroyed Cluny, not Donatello, Raphael, and Rembrandt, but the della Robbias, Pontormo, and Rococo ornament. Accordingly they favored epochs with sparse documentation and challenging gaps in evidence: the pre-Gothic Middle Ages and the early Italian Renaissance overwhelmed other fields of study to a point that, of some 48 doctoral dissertations accepted by Harvard, Yale, and Princeton before 1930, 45 were in ancient and medieval art and the remaining 3 in Italian art before 1500; European art after 1600 passed almost unnoticed before the mid-

1930's. Though most of this generation were notably urbane, they somehow recalled a frontier, adventure-seeking spirit, partly, I think, because they wanted to find channels of expression that were not simply provincial European.

The ambivalence of the relationship to Europe may explain why the unexplored field of American figurative art attracted so little attention; though it met the requirements of adventure, it was rejected as too provincial. On the other hand, American architecture, because a better case could be made for its international stature, consistently attracted able scholars (starting with Fiske Kimball, Lewis Mumford, and Henry-Russell Hitchcock) as, in the nineteenth century, it had been the only indigenous spatial art to elicit able criticism.

In the course of the 1930's the spirit that differentiated American scholars began to dissipate, and European influence increased as the field developed in size and strength, due in part to the large-scale enlistment of Europeans by American college and university faculties. While the second generation of scholars in this country had been trained by Americans either in classical archaeology or in other disciplines, few of their students completed advanced education without having worked with a distinguished foreigner. Around 1930 several German scholars were regular visitors to graduate schools on the East Coast, and the appointment of Europeans on a permanent basis was accelerated at the close of the Depression by the rapid expansion of university programs in art history and by the willingness of outstanding scholars uprooted by Hitler to take up permanent residence and citizenship in the United States.

A great majority of European teachers came from Germany, a few from France (especially to Yale University), and only an occasional visitor from Italy and England; the impact of theories and methods developed in those countries has been in the same proportion. The absence of Italians and Englishmen as representatives of their respective traditions was both a cause and an effect of the slight influence of these schools after 1920. Both were more congenial to the mood of nineteenth century art studies in this country: the predominantly Crocean Italian tradition, with its emphasis on intuition, has been too antithetical to the positivist tendency of this century to affect America deeply, in spite of the recent popularity of Italy as a locus, and Italian art as a subject, of study. The same is true of the British critical tradition—even of the new direction indicated by Clive Bell and Roger Fry—which recently has been overwhelmed even in England by the same influences that have formed American art history.[2] The preponderance of direct German influence encouraged American art historians to practice characteristically German virtues and vices. It assured a level of sophistication that contributed to an atmosphere of self-confidence, and promoted a highly refined precision in the science of historical research, so that today American and British publications in the field are more consistently reliable than those of other nations (including Germany).[3] But it also promoted a native tendency to overrate mere method and helped to widen the gap between history and criticism.

When outstanding Americans of the third generation began to publish in the early 1930's (Barr, Hitchcock, Meiss, Mumford, Schapiro, etc.), there was no longer any question of provinciality, and the "frontier" image began to disappear; they often provided leadership abroad. Members of this group, for example, did more than Europeans to raise the study of modern European art to a scholarly level.

They were less likely to devote themselves to pure connois-

[2] For an assessment of the British tradition, see John Summerson, *What Is a Professor of Fine Art?* (U. of Hull, 1961).
[3] The comparatively high standards of American scholarship are a gauge rather of economic prosperity than of superior virtue. In contrast to those in Europe, teaching and museum positions in this country are sufficiently numerous and remunerative to minimize the temptation to publish and to expertize for profit.

seurship, and were quick to see the implications of the social sciences, which had developed so rapidly in this country, for the history of art. Social, economic, even technological interpretations of art were more congenial to Americans—particularly during the Depression, when the academic world leaned to the left politically—than cultural interpretations in the sense of *Geistesgeschichte*. The affinity for this approach partially explains why a relatively large proportion of Americans chose to work in the history of architecture, the field of art most affected by socioeconomic forces. Scholars in this country have made major contributions to every epoch in the history of architecture from antiquity to the present day. The span of activity has been more restricted in the figurative arts; the third generation emerged from the Middle Ages but did not deploy about the remaining periods; the Italian Renaissance became a favored field, but the northern Renaissance, the Baroque and the eighteenth century continued to be slighted in research (exceptions: Fiske Kimball and Charles Kuhn, both significantly museum directors, and more recently G. H. Hamilton, Harold Wethey, etc; even the nineteenth century attracted little attention before the mid-1940's). Among nations, Germany and England suffered a neglect that seems inconsistent with the influence of German scholarship and the central role of English literature in the arts programs of all American universities. Finally, the sculpture of the last five-hundred years (when major achievements were mostly nonarchitectural) aroused little interest as a field of research before the 1950's.

While outstanding minds of the third generation did not openly debate problems of historical theory, they did not ignore them as had their predecessors; if it is sometimes difficult to define the approach in their work, this is due rather to purposeful eclecticism than to unclear principles. But, at the same time, the gap widened between outstanding and average performance in the field, and the volume of pedantic, formalized publication

194

and teaching was greatly increased as lesser scholars found that the newly refined methods—homegrown or imported—could be applied at will and with purely mechanical exertion to an endless number of new instances of old problems.

The third generation now provides the established leaders in teaching, the direction of museums and scholarship; their students, of just before and after World War II, constitute a fourth generation that, since it is my own, and since it is only beginning to form points of view distinguishable from those of its masters, I cannot attempt to characterize.

5

GENRES AND SCHOLARS

Underlying the great variety of approach among art historians there is a common need for certain basic information that affects every historical operation. Regardless of our philosophy of history or criticism, nearly all of us ask of the work we study: when was it done (date), where (provenance), by whom (authorship), how (materials, tools, techniques), and why (function).

The means of answering these questions are extremely varied —from the more empirical archaeological techniques described by Mr. Carpenter in his accompanying essay to the connoisseur's attribution based on sensitivity to individual artistic traits; every epoch of the past suggests a peculiar range of historical techniques—from those "dark" ages of which nothing survives but the art itself (and little of that) to recent ones that confront the student with more documentation than he can digest.

The art historian's technique for gaining information is the same as that of the archaeologist and of any other historian wherever it concerns data extrinsic to the work of art. The date, provenance, and authorship of works of art frequently may be established with the aid of inscriptions, signatures, documents preserved in archives, contemporary sources of a literary or graphic nature, or by later ("secondary") sources reflecting earlier records or preserving traditional accounts. I shall not be concerned here with this technical foundation of all historical research; like the laboratory procedures of the scientist, such methods are part of the equipment of every properly trained scholar.

The historical methods peculiar to art history are those based primarily on evidence of the sort discussed in Chapter 2, provided by works of art themselves. Where questions of date, provenance, authorship and the like are not answered by external documentation, they may be answered on the grounds of style; that is, with reference to our knowledge of the history and character of techniques, symbolic and formal conventions, and to our knowledge of the artistic personalities of individuals and groups. Accordingly, in treating the intrinsic evidence from works of art, no sharp distinction can be made between historical and critical method; indeed, where we are concerned with style, it is largely through critical processes that we arrive at historical hypotheses.

In the following pages I shall attempt to define the principal points of view in recent art history, but not simply as techniques for discovering the historical position of works of art. As mere techniques, historical and archaeological methods become obsolete at the moment of their maximum achievement. They produce propositions—such as attributions or dates—that are either right or wrong, and that become increasingly refined and precise as the number of credible propositions (those that resist challenges) increases and the number of untenable ones decreases. For a given body of information there is a limit to the productive application of any historical technique; the techniques of connoisseurship, for example, having reduced the number of paintings attributed to Giorgione from over a hundred to about a dozen, are insufficiently sensitive to solve problems of authorship that remain among those few. But historical systems are more than empirical techniques; each of them encompasses methods for eliciting the "facts," but once these methods are used to the limits of their effectiveness, history has the further function of organizing the results into images of the past.

I suggested in Chapter 3 that artistic conventions offer the most ample evidence for the study of change in style. In practice one or another type of convention is given precedence in each of the major schools of art history; formal analysis emphasizes

197

formal conventions; iconography symbolic conventions, and connoisseurship the conventions of the individual artist or group. These three schools of modern art history emerged in the second half of the nineteenth century and were given definitive formulation by outstanding European scholars at the turn of the present century. The first is associated with Heinrich Wölfflin and Alois Riegl, the second with Aby Warburg and the institute—now in London—that bears his name, with Emile Mâle, and more recently with Erwin Panofsky; and the third with the Italian amateur Giovanni Morelli, with Max Friedländer, and, in this country with Bernard Berenson. To these must be added a fourth major direction of the present century that is not rooted primarily in the evidence of art objects but rather interprets art in the light of aspects of social/cultural activity. The most effective contributions in this area have come from the school of criticism originating in Karl Marx—but exerting influence far beyond the confines of social and political thought—and the school of intellectual history exemplified by Jakob Burckhardt, Karl Justi, and by the Viennese circle of Julius Schlosser and Max Dvořák (author of *Kunstgeschichte als Geistesgeschichte*).

The borderlines between schools were more easily distinguishable in the early days of their formulation than they are today; in time the abler scholars came to see that the concepts of more than one could be employed effectively in solving a given problem. From the start there was a tendency toward the association of form analysts and connoisseurs, since the former had assumed the task of defining the historical processes of style and the latter the individual differentiations within these processes. A similar bond was established between the cultural historians and the iconographers, since the latters' search for the meaning of symbols and subject matter led directly from art into other symbol-making functions of man—myth, religion, history, politics.

Form and Style

It is mainly through the analysis of formal conventions that the character, the scope, and the behavior or styles are formulated; the great periods of the past—Byzantine, Gothic, Baroque —have been visualized in morphological terms, as representing tendencies toward certain modes of composition, of color organization, proportion, treatment of space, etc. In the early days of professional art history, formal analysis often was used as the only guide to style; today we are more aware of the complexity of the problem, and no longer try to define styles without weighing, for example, the evidence of symbolic conventions, as in iconographic studies. But formal conventions remain the pre-eminent style indicators because they tend to change continually and because, as the creation of artists alone, they are less subject to external influence than techniques or symbols, which reflect the impact of the lay technician and symbol maker. Accordingly, the most influential theories of style have been morphological. The scholars most interested in problems of form characteristically have chosen to define the nature of style change in the past: Wölfflin's influential *Principles of Art History* distinguishes Renaissance from Baroque art in terms of polar formal categories (closed versus open, linear versus painterly, plane versus recession, etc.). Riegl's major work, *Die spätrömische Kunstindustrie,* is concerned with the transition from antique to medieval form in sculpture and ornament. These and other scholars of the close of the last century, in developing a systematic technique for the analysis of formal characteristics, helped to rid the discipline and to disabuse the public of musty prejudices against certain styles of the past, among them the Baroque and the late antique.

While historians at the turn of the century aimed to define the character of such large historical epochs, the following generation sought the more subtle distinctions. In the 1920's, Wölfflin's antithesis of Renaissance-Baroque was modified, principally through the efforts of German and Austrian scholars, by the injection of a middle term: *Mannerism.* At the same time, nicer distinctions were sought in medieval art (e.g., the definition of the schools of Carolingian and post-Carolingian manuscript illumination) and the classification of art since 1800 began to take form, aided by new historical self-consciousness on the part of the artists themselves, who frequently provided the categories and the vocabulary by which their work might be discussed. The style consciousness of the early twentieth century was such that Cubism, Orphism, Fauvism, Expressionism, Futurism, Constructivism, Dadaism, and others all appeared within a decade; even the word *style* itself was adopted as a badge of honor (*Jugendstil, De Stijl*).

While the connoisseur also is concerned with defining characteristics of style largely on morphological grounds, his interest is principally in those features that differentiate personal style from that of an epoch or of a certain time and place. In practice, the characterization of epochal styles is a necessary preamble to the work of the connoisseur, as an understanding of the structure of a society is necessary for the analysis of an individual within it. Indeed, style characterization in some way underlies most art historical functions. We depend upon it to such an extent that it is difficult to keep in mind its limitations: first, that style distinctions are hypotheses and, second, that they can be made only on the grounds of conventions. Whoever deals exclusively with the conventional aspect of works of art does not encounter a central problem of criticism: the understanding and exposition of the character of individual works. This distinction is in danger of being slurred over in the teaching of art history in the colleges, where courses are organized almost invariably in terms of established epochal styles presented frequently in such rapid succession that time does not permit the instructor to represent his examples in any terms but the conventional. This results in the substitution of a primitive sort of formal analysis for meaningful criticism, a fault that vitiates the majority of current handbooks.

The approach toward style in America has been pragmatic, in the sense that scholars generally have accepted categories of style formulated abroad and have worked within the existing framework. European theoreticians of style have been influential in this country, but have not been emulated in their theoretical interests. We have contributed little to the characterization of style process in major areas of Western art: current images of Gothic, of Baroque, or of Neoclassicism, for example, were formed in Europe, and no American participated in the lively international discussion of the 1920's and 1930's that produced the concept of Mannerism, though research on the art of that era was being done in this country. In less well-trodden periods the absence of pre-existing style classifications impelled Americans into the arena of theory. C. R. Morey's effort to explain the survival of illusionism in the figurative art of the early Middle Ages led him to the creation of an "Alexandrian Style" (*Art Bulletin*, 1924), based on the hypothesis that Alexandria was the site of a vestigial survival of the mimetic tendency in late Hellenistic art. This hypothesis remained controversial among medievalists; perhaps partly because it was not so much the demonstrable characterization of a style as a bold proposition concerning the ultimate source of one.

The contribution of the United States to the literature of style has been most influential in studies on modern art, where Europeans did not have the benefit of an earlier start. This is especially true of a body of basic catalogs and monographs of the 1930's and 1940's often sponsored by museums and written by curator-scholars, such as Alfred Barr, Daniel Rich, Andrew Ritchie, James Soby, and James Sweeny (modern European

JAMES S. ACKERMAN

art; e.g., Barr's *Cubism and Abstract Art,* 1936, and *Fantastic Art, Dada, Surrealism,* 1936); and John Baur, Lloyd Goodrich, Edgar Richardson (American art). In the study of modern architecture, Lewis Mumford and Henry-Russell Hitchcock have played an especially significant role; Hitchcock's *Modern Architecture* (1929) first put the radical design of the early twentieth century into historical perspective; his study on *The International Style,* written in 1932 in collaboration with the architect Philip Johnson, established a frame for all later discussion of the new architecture. Our image of processes in the development of an indigenous American architecture has been formed in large part by Fiske Kimball, in *American Architecture* (1928) and *The Domestic Architecture of the American Colonies* (1922 and 1927); an especially stimulating formulation of the following generation is Vincent Scully's *The Shingle Style* (1953). Kimball's interest in the formulation of style concepts also produced *The Creation of the Rococo* (1943), which was the first major American study of eighteenth century art, or of French art before 1800.

Although surveys treating a whole or part of the history of Western art provide a convenient vehicle for theory and experiment in the study of style processes, they have not yet become a significant genre in American art history. Most of the more widely used handbooks have been written by university teachers whose reputation is rooted in this area rather than in independent scholarly achievements and almost all have been the receivers rather than the producers of current images of style. The second generation of American scholars were exceptional in this respect: C. R. Morey wrote handbooks on medieval and early Christian art, Kingsley Porter on medieval architecture, and Fiske Kimball, Chandler Post, and George Edgell collaborated in surveys of sculpture and architecture; but none can be classed among the more effective products of these writers, and none is still in use. Americans have not created major works

equivalent to Kenneth Clark's *The Gothic Revival,* Max Friedländer's *From Van Eyck to Breugel,* Walter Friedlaender's
David to Delacroix, or Wölfflin's *Classic Art,* to mention only
a few available in English. Recently a growing demand
from publishers and readers has encouraged more specialists
to generalize. Many of the period surveys that constitute the
forty-odd-volume "Pelican History of Art" have been assigned
to American scholars; this project, however—and others of its
kind—cannot be regarded unequivocally as a forward step in
the field. Modeled on the *Handbuch der Kunstwissenschaft* of
forty years ago and reflecting traditional tastes for the art of the
past, the program is essentially retrospective. But the ambition
to halt empirical investigation long enough to assimilate the
chaotic volume of new data and opinions that has accumulated
in the past generation appears to have increased in recent scholarship. It is reflected in the trend away from article writing
toward bookwriting, whether on general or specific themes.
Lately the principal scholarly journals in this country have
ceased to be the voice of established authorities and have
become the proving grounds for younger aspirants. The extraordinary expansion of the luxury art-book market in recent years
has brought scholars closer to the public, which is good, but it
has prodded them occasionally into rapid and facile writing,
which is bad. Few American art historians have learned to generalize on a high level.

Connoisseurship

Connoisseurship is the study of the artistic personality of an
individual artist or of a group or school of artists as revealed in
their works. It is therefore a discipline concerned not so much
with the history of style as with style in a static sense: that complex of traits common to the body of works of an individual or
group. For the connoisseur, the personal, social, and historical

causes and effects of works of art are of interest principally as an aid to their attribution and identification. His efforts may culminate in no more than the recommendation or correction of a label on a painting or an entry in a catalog, but the nature of his research, and particularly its focus on the work of art itself, is destined to draw him into subtle problems of criticism and to equip him eminently to solve them.

Bernard Berenson defined connoisseurship as "that sense of being in the presence of a given artistic personality which comes from a long intimacy." He specified the individual personality because his research and, indeed, that of the majority of scholars we call connoisseurs, was primarily in the field of Renaissance and post-Renaissance art; in other words, in that period of history in which individuality came to be cultivated to the point that personal traits become a significant factor in the production of art and are therefore clearly distinguishable from conventions common to all artists of a given time and place.

The techniques of connoisseurship rarely are applicable to works of architecture, which, since they are immovable, do not pose problems of provenance and which, since they are the collaborative products of many artisans, do not reveal idiosyncracies of personal style to the same degree as the solo arts. More readily transported artifacts, on the other hand, often get separated from external documentation of their historical position, and in such cases identification is possible only on the intrinsic physical and stylistic evidence employed by the connoisseur. Where authorship and position are established, the techniques of connoisseurship, like those of archaeology, become superfluous. Though they still provide a keen instrument of criticism, they are less in demand in studies of recent art than in those of more remote and poorly recorded eras.

Because of its material value, the art object, unlike works of literature or music, tends to attract misleading and incorrect information. Signatures, or entire works, may be forged; the

bulk of a piece may be executed by a master's assistants or emu-
lators, and original documents or contemporary sources may be
as erroneous as later commentaries. Cupidity accounts for many
historical errors; since the Renaissance, works of art have been a
kind of currency, exchangeable in the "art market." It is to the
interest of the market and consequently of collectors and
museums—whose purchases represent investments of self-
esteem as well as of money—to attribute works of art to highly
regarded artists, where this is possible without stretching the
credulity of laymen, and to resist the "demotion" of works
wrongly assigned to these artists. Our public collections still
exhibit many works generally recognized by scholars to be
incorrectly attributed. The same pressures also endow the opinion of connoisseurs with a market value; the expert whose
favorable opinion of a questionable piece can substantially
increase its price (and consequently his fee as an assessor) may
be diverted sufficiently in his search for truth to lend authority
to error. But the effects of such frailty have been minor by comparison to the massive reversal of willful confusion made possible by a century of methodical scholarship.

The connoisseur must be attentive especially to the physical
and technical aspect of the work of art, particularly in distinguishing changes in the original object wrought by time, wear,
and the handiwork of assistants and restorers. Correct assess-
ments may rest partly or wholly on the analysis of materials and
techniques. Forgeries in painting, for example, may be detected
by the discovery of pigments or of a ground that is known not to
have been used in the lifetime of the artists imitated. The scientific techniques of the restorer's laboratory, particularly photography employing frequencies beyond the visual range, often
are especially valuable to the connoisseur.

When the object of study survives in its pristine condition,
the connoisseur's attention is concentrated initially on the range
of conventions, which ordinarily provide a guide to provenance

and authorship, though there are cases—particularly where lesser artists are involved—in which even this basic objective is difficult or impossible to attain. The principal objects of interest are the individual conventions—the private traits of technique, or formal and symbolic language—that can be distinguished from those shared by other artists in the same milieu. The relation of the private complex of traits to the public can be seen in terms of the relation of an organism to its species, and the connoisseur shares with the descriptive natural scientist the technique of intricate and painstaking comparison of all available specimens. The simile is suggested by the earliest formulator of the methodology of connoisseurship, Giovanni Morelli (1816-91), who attempted to establish as a basis of attribution an exact system of classification modeled on those of the biological sciences, by categorizing such individual traits as the delineation of ears, hands, and drapery folds. The Morellian analysis, when used with the understanding that ultimately the most persuasive judgment of artistic personality is the product of a broad, synthetic criticism, was an invaluable contribution to historical method. Its technical limitation is that, within the range of conventions that an observer selects as significant or characteristic, only certain types can be classified systematically; shapes, for instance, are easier to systematize than colors and textures, and have been overemphasized by Morelli and his followers.

The connoisseur aims to establish a fixed collection of entities (the works of an artist or group) and a formula by which to characterize that collection (a definition of style embracing all the works). Both steps in this process tend to create a static and permanent image, and to the extent that this image clouds the flux of civilization and the passing of time, the connoisseur is nonhistorical. He is interested in the processes of style changes chiefly as external factors reflected in an individual style, and within the individual style he seeks to discover the cohesive factors rather than to explain the dynamics of change. Berenson's term *the artistic personality*—roughly a synonym for the individual style—conveys the image of an entity as integrated and isolated as the human personality, whereas for historical purposes it is useful to visualize style as being as fluid and as communicable as language. This tendency of connoisseurship to isolate styles also contributed in the past to the image of "schools" of art fashioned—often arbitrarily—along national, regional, or communal lines. Probably the rise of connoisseurship, with its emphasis in the uniqueness of the "personality" or locale, was related to the rugged individualism, free enterprise, and nationalism of the later nineteenth century.

Berenson's way of getting the "long intimacy" with original works of art that he believed to be a qualification for connoisseurship was to live in Italy, where the objects of his study were concentrated. The connoisseur's need for constant renewal of acquaintance with originals makes regular travel a condition of his occupation, and favors museum employment over academic, since museums offer uninterrupted contact with at least some works of art, and since the selection of objects for purchase places a premium on the skills of the connoisseur. So Americans are at a disadvantage as connoisseurs. We have fine museums, but Europe remains the locus for the study of European art, and American art is such a recent development that it offers only a limited scope for the techniques of connoisseurship. Further, so few of our museums support research as a major function of curatorial personnel that scholars generally prefer positions in colleges and universities where, however, except at the highest level, connoisseurship proves to be the least amenable of art historical techniques to instruction: "long intimacy" cannot be taught. Yet, in spite of the obstacles, a few Americans have ranked among the outstanding connoisseurs of European, especially Italian, art. Berenson's achievements in clarifying the general outlines of authorship in fifteenth and sixteenth century Italian painting were monumental. Two catalogs represent his most significant contribution: *The Drawings of the Florentine Painters* (1903), and *Italian Pictures of the Renaissance* (1932). The latter, simply a list of the major painters and the works that the author assigns to them, is the distillation of a lifetime of observation. Much of it has been supplanted, and nearly every specialist grumbles about its inadequacies, but among scholars throughout the world it has been a foundation and a stimulus in the continuing search for precision over the ensuing thirty years.

Berenson and his contemporaries prepared foundations for a more intensive and refined science of connoisseurship in the following generation, as represented in this country by the teaching and publications of Richard Offner, whose *Corpus of Florentine Painting* (1931-   , in progress) has undertaken to assign every known Florentine picture—to date, only of the earlier fourteenth century—to a known or forgotten master or to the circle of one of these; the author has of necessity regularly spent over half of each year in Florence. Offner represents connoisseurship in its purest form; "a history of art," he wrote as he began the *Corpus,* "or any portion of it, should be evolved directly out of its concrete examples [and] . . . these, primarily, should give shape to the historic panorama. Such an approach differs in emphasis rather than in kind. It studies the work of art more exclusively for its style as radical for historical conclusion, and puts it above the testimony of written records."

Few, if any, of the younger scholars have continued the Berenson-Offner tradition of pure connoisseurship; the remaining problems of attribution are progressively less urgent and interesting as the work of major artists is clarified, and problems that resist solution by "long intimacy" may respond to treatment by iconographical analysis or by a variety of other techniques. Yet the tradition reinforces a number of major studies of recent years—principally in Italian Renaissance art—such as those of Millard Meiss (*Painting in Florence and Siena After the Black Death,* 1951), Sydney Freedberg (*Parmigianino,* 1950; *Painting of the High Renaissance in Rome and Florence,* 1961), H. W. Janson (*The Sculpture of Donatello,* 1957), and Frederick Hartt (*Giulio Romano,* 1958). Paul J. Sachs, one of America's most influential connoisseurs, and the pre-eminent educator of museum personnel between the two world wars, is known in publications chiefly through the exemplary *Catalog of Drawings in the Fogg Museum* (1946), written with his colleague Agnes Mongan. An opinionated but exceptional incursion of the methods of Renaissance connoisseurship into the study of modern painting is the work of the collector Albert C. Barnes (e.g., *The Art of Renoir,* 1935, with Violette de Mazia), who was inspired by John Dewey's theory of art.

The concentration of American connoisseurs of the third generation in the field of Italian Renaissance art is as inexplicable as the fascination of their elders with medieval Spain. Before 1950 American authors produced no important books and a mere handful of articles on French, Flemish, English, Dutch, or German art between medieval and modern times. Very recently the perspective of younger scholars has broadened to encompass all those areas.

The scholar who places the work of art "above the testimony of written records" must be an especially sensitive critic of visual form; he must have "an eye," as the connoisseurs say. This attainment is not accessible to everyone, nor is it, except among the most gifted individuals, a quite reliable basis of scholarship. Most American historians have taken a more pragmatic approach to problems of attribution, seeking out the tangible evidence of documents and restricting their commentary on "artistic personality" to the analysis of conventions. In this category belong some substantial contributions to our knowledge of the past, beginning with the work of two pioneers in the development of graduate education in the United States, the della Robbia catalogs (1912-22) by Alan Marquand and the exhaustive chronicle of Spanish Renaissance painting (1930-58, left incomplete at the death of the author) by Chandler Post.

Documentary scholarship in architectural history has been particularly able, both in the medieval field, in which the methods of classical archaeology have been employed in excavation, and in laying the foundation for our knowledge of nineteenth and twentieth century architecture. Early contributions to the field were made at the close of the nineteenth century by Charles H. Moore in his volumes on Gothic and Renaissance architecture; a friend of Charles Eliot Norton, Moore made the last strong statement of the Ruskinian tradition. Basic medieval studies have been those of H. C. Butler (Princeton University archaeological expeditions to Syria, 1914 ff.; *Early Churches in Syria,* 1929), Kingsley Porter (*Lombard Architecture,* 1915-17), Kenneth Conant (a quarter-century of articles on the monastic churches at Cluny, summarized in his *Carolingian and Romanesque Architecture, 800-1200, 1959*), Sumner Crosby (*The Abbey of St. Denis,* 1942), and George Forsyth (*The Church of St. Martin at Angers,* 1953). The work of Henry-Russell Hitchcock exemplifies rare precision and thoroughness in the study of the architecture of the past 150 years (monographs on H. H. Richardson, 1936, Frank Lloyd Wright, 1942; *Early Victorian Architecture in Britain,* 1954; other valuable contributions in this area have been made by Talbot Hamlin, Hugh Morrison, and C. L. V. Meeks). By contrast to the situation in the study of painting, interest in Renaissance and Baroque architecture has been awakened only recently (Harold Wethey, *Colonial Architecture and Sculpture in Peru,* 1949; George Kubler, *Aquitectura de los siglos XVII y XVIII [Ars Hispaniae,* XIV] 1957; David Coffin, *The Villa d'Este at Tiv-*

oli, 1960; J. S. Ackerman, *The Architecture of Michelangelo,* 1961).

Much of the American contribution to the study of nineteenth and twentieth century painting belongs to the documentary genre; the art of recent times is recorded sufficiently to reduce problems of attribution to a minor position and to make the study of sources especially rewarding.

Iconography

For the sake of clarity I arbitrarily have put the analyst of form and the connoisseur into one class as contrasted to another composed of the iconographer and the social historian. The first group is concerned more with the formal conventions of style, the second with the symbolic conventions. Formal conventions in any art are characteristic of that art alone, so the first group tends to focus attention on evidence provided primarily or exclusively by works of art; but communication in symbols is characteristic of many forms of human intercourse, so the second group tends to focus attention on the relation between works of art and other activities of society. The iconographer studies this relation in terms of the specific meanings conveyed by the artist's imagery, while the social historian tends to encompass the broader problems of the role of art in society.[1]

For the greater part of history, works of art have been made with the intention of recalling to the observer some specific image of a religious, philosophical, literary, or historical origin. Only a limited understanding of the art of the past would be possible if we were not able to preserve and to reconstruct these images—narratives from the Bible and Apocrypha, the scholastic theologians' structure of the heavenly hierarchy, the neo-

[1] See Erwin Panofsky, "Iconography and Iconology: An Introduction to the Study of Renaissance Art" in *Studies in Iconology* (Oxford, 1939; pp. 3-31) (Harper [Torchbooks], 1962).

Platonic characterization of love, themes from Ovid's *Metamorphoses,* or the circumstances of the murder of Marat.

The reading and understanding of symbols occurs on several levels; it takes a specific kind of experience to recognize that a seated lady with a child on her lap and two or three differently dressed men to her left and right represents the Madonna and saints; more specialized learning is required to identify the nude man with an arrow protruding from his chest as St. Sebastian and the man wearing a cardinal's red hat and accompanied by a lion as St. Jerome, and to realize that the group represented is composed into an altarpiece of a type called the santa conversazione. Making identifications of this kind is the task of the iconographer, but he does not stop with a mere glossary of attributes and types. His most compelling task is in the sphere of what Erwin Panofsky has called iconology, in which the theme and its treatment are interpreted as manifestations of the intellectual and spiritual posture of an age. Such interpretation demands the re-creation of the significance of the santa conversazione for its time and place, and for our understanding of the religious and artistic attitude that caused the once-isolated saints and Madonna—no two of them historically contemporary—to be brought together into a social relationship. The iconologist deals with the themes of images much as the literary critic deals with characterization, action, and imagery in drama.

Often the meaning of an image is revealed not only by reference to sources outside the visual arts, but by comparison with other like images (and in the art of recent times this often is the only guide to meaning); a certain theme may appear in a group of works produced during a few years or over the span of generations or centuries. In the latter case the iconographer, like the historian of style, may be interested less in the interpretation of its appearance in a particular work than in the significance for intellectual history of the processes of change in the presentation of the theme itself. He would study, that is, the different forms taken by a theme—such as the equestrian statue, the crucifixion, or the still life—that survives successive changes of style. This aspect of iconography reminds us that, historically speaking, content has not always been coextensive with form; not only have some themes persisted through millennia but some styles have survived radical changes of theme— far into the Middle Ages the Hellenistic style was adapted to Christian imagery.

The perfect iconographer would require an encyclopedic knowledge of the culture in which he works. For the study of European and Mediterranean art since the time of Christ he would have to be familiar not only with the vast body of Western literature, philosophy, theology, history, and all other records of human achievements in that period itself, but nearly everything that preceded it; for the Old Testament and the records of Greece and Rome have inspired artists up to the present day; indeed, the history of Western art since antiquity might be represented as an extended effort to accommodate in one system the Hebraic-Christian and the classical-pagan traditions. This achievement is far beyond anyone's reach; like many other scholars, the iconographer must be satisfied with seeking to learn where to look for what he does not know. Even at that, he needs more specialized skills than most art historians; languages are especially important, and Latin, Greek, and several modern languages are essential. The fact that American secondary education is deficient in linguistic training—particularly in the classics—and generally below European standards in literary and historical studies, partly explains the small number of important contributions to the iconographical literature from this side of the Atlantic.

Iconographic studies are not restricted to the arts capable of narration, but can be useful in interpreting any artifact capable of conveying ideas. Architecture is a particularly rewarding field for research in symbolism, for the mechanism of architectural revival is explicable principally in symbolic terms. Through the ages, the several parts of buildings have accumulated specific meanings; from earliest times the dome has been associated with the heavens, and for centuries domes were decorated with stars in the most diverse cultures; the tower stood for secular power; medieval and Renaissance baptisteries were octagonal because the number 8 stood for resurrection; in the twentieth century sheer planes of glass and white plaster have symbolized "honesty" and "progress" and, to signify mechanical speed, even stationary structures and objects have been "streamlined."

The methods of iconography also are suited to the study of theoretical or technical aspects of art that are at once symbolic and formal. Among these are perspective, which Panofsky has called symbolic form, and proportion—interrelated disciplines that are culturally determined and therefore have a history.

Iconography raises special problems not encountered in ordinary criticism. While the critic is concerned primarily with the actual effect of the work of art itself, the iconographer is after what the artist and his patrons meant it to say. In this sense, criticism aims at interpretation, but iconographical analysis, particularly where it involves the proposal of specific sources for symbols, motives, or themes, culminates in historical propositions that can be only right or wrong. So the optimal support for iconographical analysis of a work is an established and documented iconic tradition or a statement by the artist of his intention; next best is the evidence of contemporaries. Where all of these are absent, it often is necessary to make inferences based on one's knowledge and intuitions about the intellectual processes of the artist and his times. This procedure is comparable to the intuitive approach of connoisseurs to attribution, but it is likely to be less trustworthy. The evidence of an artist's "hand" and habits of composition are far more concrete than the evidence of his intellectual processes. There are, for example, several interpretations of the meaning of the tympanum at Vézelay, Botticelli's *Primavera,* or Velázquez' *Los Borrachos,* and the better ones, though mutually exclusive, are equally credible. Thus an identification of the symbolic sources of a work of art may be learned, profound, a significant contribution to intellectual history, and be both wrong and irrelevant to the work under investigation. (The connoisseur may be equally wrong, but the justification of his attribution must be relevant to the work.) This possibility, arising from the extrinsic nature of the iconographer's sources and evidence, is the hazard of specialized scholarship in this area—a hazard that may be overcome, as the more gifted scholars have shown, by integrating iconographic and formal studies into an ampler sphere of criticism.

Two phases of interest in iconography may be found in American art history. The first, in which subject matter is used principally as a clue to identification, dating, etc., is identified with the Princeton school, and particularly with C. R. Morey; the second, reflecting the influence of European "iconology," made its appearance only after 1930. Neither phase emphasized the study of symbolic conventions as a distinct art historical philosophy, as some Europeans had done; in the first, it was a quantitative tool (iconography as an index of morphology), and in the second it was assimilated into other approaches: few Americans could be identified as iconographers, though iconographical method gradually has become an integral part of the training and practice of American scholars.

In the Princeton school, iconography took the form of a systematic study of symbolic convention modeled (consciously?) on linguistic-philological methods. As the basic instrument for this study, the Index of Christian Art was founded at Princeton in 1917.[2] The index is a huge card catalog of reproductions of medieval figurative art—major and minor—organized and cross-referenced by a staff of specialists according to the subjects depicted; students throughout the world use the index for information on the incidence of appearance of a certain saint, a symbol, of depictions of the holy sepulchre, or the like. In attempting to solve problems of provenance and chronology in early medieval art, the scholars of the second generation at Princeton employed iconographical evidence of this kind together with the analysis of formal conventions (as: E. B. Smith, *Early Christian Iconography and a School of Ivory Carvers in Provence,* 1918; A. M. Friend, "Carolingian Art in the Abbey of St. Denis," *Art Studies,* 1923; C. R. Morey, *Early Christian Art,* 1942). Princeton only occasionally produced overtly iconographical studies (J. Carson Webster, *The Labors of the Months in Antique and Mediaeval Art,* 1938; E. B. Smith, *Architectural Symbolism of Imperial Rome and the Middle Ages,* 1956).

More recently (1949; 1956) the Institute of Fine Arts of New York University, in collaboration with the Warburg Institute in London, has instituted two programs for the systematic collection of visual sources of use not only in iconographic studies, but for a broad range of historical research: the Census of Antique Works of Art Known to Artists of the Renaissance, and a photographic corpus of the history of engraving and etching (cf. a study by the director of the former project, Phyllis Bober, *Drawings After the Antique by Amico Aspertini,* 1957). Scholars at the Institute of Fine Arts have published iconographic reference works (e.g., Dorothy C. Shorr, *The Christ Child in Devotional Images in Italy During the XIV Century,* 1954; Mirella Levi d'Ancona, *The Iconography of the*

[2] Helen Woodruff, *The Index of Christian Art at Princeton University* (Princeton, 1942).

Immaculate Conception in the Middle Ages and Early Renaissance, 1957).

Thirty years ago European iconography as exemplified by the Warburg Institute was introduced into this country by its most distinguished advocate, Erwin Panofsky. A number of students who were not to become iconographic specialists nevertheless assimilated the methods and did some writing exclusively within the genre (Millard Meiss, "The Madonna of Humility," *Art Bulletin*, 1936; Meyer Schapiro, "Cain's Jaw-Bone That Did the First Murder," *Art Bulletin*, 1942; Frederick Hartt, "Lignum Vitae in Medio Paradisi, The Stanza d'Eliodoro and the Sistine Ceiling," *Art Bulletin*, 1950; H. W. Janson, *Apes and Ape-Lore in the Middle Ages and Renaissance*, 1952). Studies in medieval symbolism initiated at the Warburg Institute in London by Fritz Saxl have been carried on in this country by Harry Bober (e.g., "The Zodiacal Miniature of the Très Riches Heures of the Duke of Berry," *Journal of the Warburg and Courtauld Institutes*, 1948).

Students of art since 1800 have adapted iconographical techniques to the quite different demands of the modern period (Lorenz Eitner, "The Open Window and the Storm-tossed Boat," *Art Bulletin*, 1955; Robert Rosenblum, "The Origin of Painting: A Problem in the Iconology of Romantic Classicism," *Art Bulletin*, 1957). In lectures at Columbia University, Meyer Schapiro pioneered in the application of psychoanalytic method to the interpretation of the personalized imagery of twentieth century art.

Social History of Art

In defining the province of the art historian, I suggested that his primary data are works of art. The strict connoisseur and historian of style is interested almost exclusively in these data; he finds other historical materials useful mainly to the extent that they help to reveal the immediate circumstances of production by documenting authorship, the time and place of production, and the availability of other works that may have influenced the production. Where there is some conflict between inferences drawn from the work of art and from written documents, he tends to favor the former. He is unlikely to be concerned with the biography or psychology of the artist or the role of the patron or of the society by and for whom a work was conceived, except when such information is conveyed specifically —as may happen in a portrait—by the work itself. This limitation implies the belief that works of art are sufficiently distinct products of human activity to warrant historical treatment primarily on the grounds of their own internal evidence and independent of other aspects of civilization.

Some historians who do not accept the restriction of the field to the sphere of works of art have sought to explain aspects of style and historical processes partly or wholly in terms of the action of external forces in society. Their theories may be discussed under the heading of the social history of art, which embraces approaches based on the principles of intellectual history and of the social sciences—political history, sociology, economics, psychology, and anthropology.[3] Although the social history of art gained its greatest boost from the rising status of the social sciences during the first half of the twentieth century, its origins can be traced to the start of professional activity in the field. In Burckhardt's *The Civilization of the Renaissance in Italy* (1860), art is discussed as an aspect of a historical revolution. In the scattered references of Karl Marx and Friedrich Engels, it became a weapon and a measuring rod of economic and class struggle; and in Karl Justi it appeared as the product of a cultural milieu embracing a variety of intellectual activities

[3] On the social history of art and related theories, see the penetrating criticism of Arnold Hauser in *The Philosophy of Art History* (Knopf, 1959).

(*Diego Velázquez und sein Jahrhundert,* 1888). These directions came to a focus within the field at the turn of the century, particularly in the Vienna school as represented by Alois Riegl (who suggested a somewhat contradictory combination of social and purely formal determinants of change in style), Julius Schlosser and Max Dvořák. The initiators of the new technique of iconography, notably Aby Warburg, visualized their specialty as closely related to social history (e.g., *Bildniskunst und florentinisches Bürgertum,* 1902).

This new point of view arose partly in reaction to connoisseurs and historians of style who defined the history of art as a closed system motivated primarily by artists out of personal experience. That system was a legacy of the economic separation of the artist from society symbolized by the rise of the museum and sanctified by the romantic artist myth; it would have been inconceivable during the vast ages of history when art was thought of not as an embellishment but as a necessity of life. Today it seems self-evident that wherever a work of art is produced to serve a specific and indispensable function, and its conventions are influenced in some way by the consumer, it can be evaluated and understood better in the light of knowledge of the institution or individual(s) for whom it was made. This is especially true of architecture, which comes into being as a vessel of social organizations; a building cannot be properly understood apart from the society that forms it and that it in turn helps to form. But the social history of art is not justified only in the criticism of patently "necessary" art; the social sciences have provided so broad a view of psychological and social function that all art, no matter how esoteric or how much for-art's-sake, may be interpreted as fulfilling the needs of some segment of society as well as of the individual artist.

A peculiar virtue of the social history of art is that it bridges barriers that separate historical disciplines. When we interpret a work of art in terms of the conditions that brought it into being, we call upon sources that art has in common with the other activities of society. While the problem of establishing the place of origin of a Carolingian miniature can be discussed only among art historians, the impact of the Counterreformation on intellectual life is a viable theme for a symposium of art historians, musicologists, philosophers, historians, and others. Further, certain parallels between, say, the literature and the painting of a given time may help to illuminate some difficult aspect of the latter, particularly at moments when artists themselves are preoccupied with literature. The study of relationships of this sort is a prerequisite for the interpretation of art theory and criticism in past eras: the understanding of Leonardo da Vinci's treatise on painting requires a knowledge of Renaissance studio practice, but also of the science, philosophy, and classical learning of the period. For such reasons, the social history of art has appealed to educators and scholars as an antidote to specialization and as a means of giving the study of art a "broad humanistic basis."

But these benefits often have been gained at the expense of important functions of art history. Since the several disciplines can be brought together only by focusing on common denominators among them, the attention of the social historian is necessarily drawn away from the individual character and quality, the uniqueness, of particular works of art. When this occurs, the historian's prime object is no longer the work of art; it becomes the social situation or institution. If I were to collaborate with colleagues in other fields in a discussion of the Counterreformation, I would choose works of art as documents of a social-religious movement; my standard of selection would be neither artistic excellence nor significance of style, but relevance to the edicts of the Council of Trent or to the writings of St. Carlo Borromeo. Perhaps the majority of examples would be inferior works by obscure masters, because the best artists were neither controlled by nor reacting against church edicts and institutions. In short, had I been interested primarily in art for its own sake I might have avoided the area entirely, just because it was so barren of creative talent. A study of Counterreformation art may make an important contribution to the history of ideas, but it is not so much the contribution of an art historian as of a social historian employing works of art as documents for the investigation of an institution. The Counterreformation is not exceptional in this respect; social milieu often is revealed better in inferior works of art than in masterpieces, which owe their distinction not to the fact that they reveal more of their origins but, on the contrary, to the fact that their message is universally valid, for any time and place. In short, historians do not necessarily broaden our perspective or contribute to the enrichment of humanistic studies by divesting art "documents" of the qualities that are peculiar to works of art and that differentiate them from other products of society.

If works of art are documents for the social historian, they are weapons for the social reformer and revolutionary. In Marxist theory, which has been the most influential of its kind, art, like all other products of the imagination, provides an arsenal for the struggle of social-economic classes; so styles of the past are associated with, and in essence attributed to, the class that patronized or supported them. But since the reformer uses history to promote contemporary social action, he cannot merely indicate the socioeconomic forces operating on and aided by the art of the past, but must demonstrate which forces represented progress toward and which a retreat from his desired goal; it is understood from the start that his evaluation of the art corresponds to his evaluation of the forces. Whatever may be said of Marxist criticism as a social weapon in its own right, it involves a fundamental conflict in values by making aesthetic judgments on the grounds of the efficacy of works of art as social propaganda. Moreover, it has flaws as a historical method, since it is often difficult to associate style with class without forming arbitrary distinctions, and since our image of social structures in all but the recent past is clouded and constantly changing.

These reservations, however, apply to extreme versions of the social history of art; they are not meant to discredit important contributions of social history and criticism in the past or to underrate its potential value now and in the future. If the study of the impact of society on art is used as a function of the study of art itself—if scholars are drawn to, rather than by, the study of society—our understanding of the art of the past can be only enriched; indeed, it is the most effective means of expanding the parochial vision of historians of style and connoisseurs.

Henry Adams's *Mont-Saint-Michel and Chartres* (1905; posthumously published in 1913), perhaps the earliest American example of the social-intellectual genre, has been read more widely than any book of its kind; but because it belongs rather to the tradition of Michelet and Ruskin than to professional historical scholarship, it produced no following among early art historians. Nor did the *Geistesgeschichte* of the Vienna school affect American writers before the mid-1930's. The first stirrings of social interest appear in the work of Kingsley Porter and Lewis Mumford. In Porter's *Romanesque Sculpture of the Pilgrimage Roads* (1923), social criteria (the principle that affinities of style in monuments scattered through France and Spain might be attributed to chains of communication along the routes set out for the medieval pilgrim) apparently emerged from the evidence of the monuments rather than being adopted from the start as a modus operandi. By contrast, Mumford's history of American architecture, *Sticks and Stones* (1924), together with *The Brown Decades* (1931) and later works, used historical method to urge contemporary social and architectural reform by adjusting techniques of Marxist criticism to the purposes of what might be called a radical humanism. ("I have not sought to criticize particular buildings or tendencies: I have tried rather by approaching our modern problems from the historic side to criticize the forces that . . . have conditioned our architecture.") Mumford's method was grounded in the philosophy of the Scotsman Patrick Geddes and of the American architect Louis Sullivan; his scheme of the main currents in American architecture and even his aesthetic evaluations made their mark on every subsequent contribution to the field (including those of European scholars).

The orthodox Marxist system, though virtually ignored by writers in this country, was adopted in one historical work, Milton Brown's *The Painting of the French Revolution* (1938); because few periods in history are so well suited to treatment in terms of class struggle, Brown was able to apply Marxian principles with less of the distortion and omission than are found in many European and Russian contributions to the socialist literature of art (cf. one of the best of these, Frederick Antal's *Florentine Painting and Its Social Background,* 1948). Though the Marxist approach accelerated the growth of American interest in social history, especially during the Depression, it has been used as a specific historical method far less than in other fields of the humanities. Not, I should say, because the history of art has been philosophically conservative, but because it has been antiphilosophical.

The tendency to study the history of American art as an aspect of political, social, and intellectual history is strong even among non-Marxist scholars; this is particularly true where the stature of the art is not sufficiently high to sustain intensive examination of the intrinsic character of the works themselves. In Oliver Larkin's *Art and Life in America* (1949), the most widely used survey of its kind, works of art are used as documents of stages of civilization in this country. Edgar Richardson's *Washington Allston* (1948) studies the artist in the light of an intellectual milieu; in "Religious Expression in American Architecture" (*Religion in American Life,* 1961), Donald Egbert examines American church design in the light of the theological background; John Coolidge's *Mill and Mansion: A Study of Architecture and Society in Lowell, Massachusetts* (1942) and Anthony Garvan's *Architecture and Town Planning in Colonial Connecticut* (1951) study early American society through its buildings.

Outside the American field, leading scholars of the third generation were able, after 1935, to assimilate the techniques of social and intellectual history into a more comprehensive approach that no longer interfered with a penetrating criticism of works of art. Outstanding examples, representing a major and independent contribution of American scholarship to art historical methodology, were published by George Kubler and Millard Meiss. Kubler's *Mexican Architecture of the Sixteenth Century* (1948) employs the methods of demography, ecology, economic and technological history as a background for an intensive study of the individual monuments. In *Painting in Florence and Siena After the Black Death* (1951), Meiss brings his background as a connoisseur and iconographer into partnership with a study of religious and literary history to explain a dramatic shift in style following the plagues of the mid-fourteenth century in central Italy. A chapter from the intellectual history of modern times is studied with perception in Robert Goldwater's *Primitivism in Modern Painting* (1938), which traces the evolution of the taste for primitive and child art and its impact on the art of this century. The chief published evidence of the influential methodology developed by Meyer Schapiro for the study of modern art, with its close ties to the social sciences, is found in the text of two albums of colored plates, *Vincent van Gogh* (1950) and *Paul Cézanne* (1952).

The influence of anthropology on the history of art has been negligible except in those fields, such as primitive art, in which historians have turned to anthropologists as collectors of objects and of information. A collaboration on a theoretical level remains almost untried, although directions have been suggested by A. L. Kroeber (*Configurations of Culture Growth,* 1944), Dagobert Frey (*Kunstwissenschaftliche Grundfragen,* 1946), and George Kubler (*The Shape of Time,* 1962). Anthropological techniques could assist comparative studies in the art of different cultures (e.g., affinities of ornamental motives or architectural structure between unrelated societies) or of different social structures in the same culture; of the dynamics of artistic production (e.g., why some periods are more favorable than others to the arts; how the vitality of the spatial arts relates to that of other arts), or of shifts in the interrelationships among the spatial arts (why architecture is dominant in one culture, painting or sculpture in another); of the impact of artistic forms on other cultural forms such as fashion and mores, or of the role of race, nationality, and climate in the making of art.

Psychoanalysis also has had little direct influence on art historical practice, but for a different reason. Frequent attempts have been made to use psychoanalytic technique in the interpretation of the art of the past, particularly in the analysis of symbolic conventions (cf. Walter Abel, *The Collective Dream in Art,* 1957), but with little success from a historical or critical viewpoint. The investigation of unconscious processes for obvious reasons has concentrated on the study and treatment of living subjects and has not yet achieved a sound—much less a scientific—approach to historical material (see Meyer Schapiro's penetrating criticism in "Leonardo and Freud," *Journal of the History of Ideas,* 1956). To the extent that psychoanalysis has affected all aspects of contemporary thought, however, it has influenced the history and particularly the criticism of art. More functional assistance has come from direction of clinical psychology, which has prompted two theoretical works of basic importance for criticism: Rudolf Arnheim's *Art and Visual Perception* (1954) and E. H. Gombrich's *Art and Illusion* (1960).

Typological studies, in which a motif, a genre, or a technique is studied in varied historical contexts—for example, the nude, still-life painting, etching—have rarely been produced in America, though they appear frequently abroad. (Two notable American works are Clarence Ward's *Mediaeval Church Vaulting,* 1915, and E. B. Smith's *The Dome,* 1950.)

While disinterest in philosophical problems and the difficulty of working with original sources in foreign collections accounts for the rarity of American criticism of texts on art theory, the few contributions have been of high quality: Rensselaer Lee's "Ut Pictura Poesis," *Art Bulletin* (1940), is a fundamental study of major themes in classical European theory of the sixteenth and seventeenth centuries; Meyer Schapiro has written a penetrating essay on medieval theory ("On the Aesthetic Attitude in Romanesque Art," *Art and Thought,* 1947). In an intensive study of the sources relating to Rembrandt, Seymour Slive brushed away fundamental misconceptions relating to the artist's career (*Rembrandt and His Critics, 1630-1730,* 1953). The archaeologist W. B. Dinsmoor published an exemplary study on "The Literary Remains of Sebastiano Serlio," *Art Bulletin* (1942). Basic studies on the sources of nineteenth and twentieth century art recently have become more numerous, as: Joseph C. Sloane, *French Painting Between the Past and the Present* (1951); G. H. Hamilton, *Manet and His Critics* (1954); Christopher Gray, *Cubist Aesthetic Theories* (1953); Norman Schlenoff, *Ingres, ses sources littéraires: Cahiers littéraires inédits* (1956).

Insufficient effort has been made by American scholars and publishers to make available in critical editions, facsimiles, reprints, or translations the basic documentary and literary sources of art history. University press publications such as Princeton's

Leonardo da Vinci's Treatise on Painting (ed. A. P. MacMahon, 1956) and Yale's *Alberti on Painting* (trans. John Spencer, 1956) are rare. A more vigorous effort has been made by Wittenborn and Schultz, Inc., a dealer, in publishing a series, "Documents of Modern Art" (ed. Robert Motherwell), of reprints and translations of important twentieth century sources.

Conclusion

One of the great deficiencies of art historical study in this most highly industrialized society is, paradoxically, the absence of efficient organizations for the procurement and distribution of the essential tools of education and scholarship. This is particularly notable in respect to visual materials: photographs and lantern slides. Thousands of institutions in America annually duplicate effort and expenditure to acquire and to reproduce material, much of which is of a quality substantially inferior to what could be obtained by collaborative effort. When fine photographic negatives are procured by scholars and institutions, they are not preserved in any central repository for general use; educational centers have not been able to benefit from the vast photographic files assembled by commercial publishers and journals; expert photographers public spirited enough to travel abroad or within this country to record monuments have no lines of communication to eager consumers in the universities, and rarely are able to realize the expenses of a voyage, much less a reimbursement for their labor. Foundations have been reluctant to support photographic campaigns, with the notable exception of the Carnegie Corporation's sponsorship of the production of a set of color slides of American art. Furthermore, photographic repositories such as those of the Frick Art Reference Library or of the Fogg Art Museum of Harvard University are composed almost entirely of prints purchased from commercial distributors and bound by copyright, so that they cannot be reproduced for the use of scholars elsewhere in the country. The same problem hampers the distribution of microfilms of scholarly source material.

A similar situation exists in the organization of bibliographical tools. The great cost of illustrated books on the arts constitutes an excessively heavy burden on our libraries, yet no plan for sharing the cost has been considered. Thousands of books, pamphlets, and journals, such as the annals of provincial European antiquarian societies, or publications in languages inaccessible to the majority of scholars in the field, are sufficiently esoteric that one copy would serve the nation, if only we could agree to distribute the responsibility for acquisition equitably.

Finally, our bibliographical indexing systems are quite inadequate. There is no record of current book publication in the field, and the principal source of information on periodical literature, *The Art Index,* limits its coverage to this country and to an arbitrarily selected portion of the major journals elsewhere.

❦

I could not hope to be objective in discussing a subject to which I am so close; what I have said about the practice of art history in America is partly an extension of my preceding argument for what I termed "contextual" method. By this I mean that the work of art must be examined in its total context: cultural, historical, physical, psychological, formal, symbolic—that any information or impression that relates to it in any way may prove to be relevant to historical-critical study. I have represented art history in America as evolving from nineteenth century amateurism toward a phase of fragmentation into specialized techniques in the first half of the twentieth century—independently at the start, later under European influence; finally,

I have detected and applauded the emergence, in work of a few outstanding scholars at midcentury, of a comprehensive principle in which the isolated techniques of the preceding generation began to fuse in a more penetrating criticism. This development is not a mere eclecticism following a phase of pioneering in method; eclecticism would imply the artificial agglomeration of elements from diverse sources, and this could not be achieved in terms of our earlier systems—the social historian and the connoisseur, the student of form and the student of content, had almost no points of contact. The fusion of which I have spoken is attainable only by anchoring investigation in the work of art. When the work is the primary datum, all of the traditional historical methods may be employed together; they are harmonized, interwoven, through their relation to it.

≈≶≷≈

A SHORT BIBLIOGRAPHY

Antal, Frederick, "Remarks on the Method of Art History," *Burlington Magazine,* XCI (1949), 49-52; 73-75.

Berenson, Bernard, *Aesthetics and History in the Visual Arts.* New York: Pantheon Books, Inc., 1948.

Croce, Benedetto, *Aesthetic as Science of Expression and General Linguistic,* 2nd ed. New York: Noonday Press, 1953; Peter Smith, 1960.

————, *La Critica e la storia delle arti figurative.* Bari: Gius. Laterza & Figli, 1934, 1946.

Ettlinger, L. D., *Art History Today.* London: University College, 1961.

Foçillon, Henri, *The Life of Forms in Art,* 2nd ed. New York: George Wittenborn, Inc., 1948.

Frankl, Paul, *Das System der Kunstwissenschaft.* Brünn/Leipzig: R. M. Rohrer, 1938.

Friedländer, Max, *On Art and Connoisseurship.* New York: Beacon Press, 1960.

Frye, Northrop, *Anatomy of Criticism.* Princeton: Princeton University Press, 1957.

Gombrich, Ernst Hans, "Psychoanalysis and the History of Art," *International Journal of Psychoanalysis,* XXXIV (1954). (Reprinted in *Freud and the Twentieth Century,* ed. Benjamin N. Nelson. New York: Meridian Books, Inc., 1957; Peter Smith, 1958.)

————, *Art and Scholarship.* London: University College, 1957. (Reprinted in *College Art Journal,* XVII [1958].)

————, *Art and Illusion.* New York: Pantheon Books, Inc., 1960.

Hauser, Arnold, *The Philosophy of Art History.* New York: Alfred A. Knopf, Inc., 1959.

Ivins, William Mills, *Prints and Visual Communication.* Cambridge: Harvard University Press, 1953.

Kubler, George, *The Shape of Time.* New Haven: Yale University Press, 1962.

Langer, Susanne K., *Problems of Art.* New York: Charles Scribner's Sons, 1957.

Malraux, André, *The Voices of Silence.* New York: Doubleday & Co., Inc., 1953.

Pächt, Otto, "Art Historians and Art Critics—VI: Alois Riegl," *Burlington Magazine,* CV (1963).

Panofsky, Erwin, "Uber das Verhältnis der Kunstgeschichte zum Kunsttheorie," *Zeitschrift für Ästhetik,* XVIII (1924-25).

————, "Zum Problem der Beschreibung and Inhaltsdeutung von Werken der bildenden Kunst," *Logos,* XXI (1932).

————, "The History of Art as a Humanistic Discipline" in *Meaning in the Visual Arts.* New York: Doubleday & Co., Inc. (Anchor Books), 1955.

Riegl, Alois, *Stilfragen.* Berlin: Georg Siemens, 1893.

————, *Die spätrömische Kunst-industrie.* Vienna: K. K. Hof- und Staatsdruckerei, 1901; 2nd ed., 1927.

Schapiro, Meyer, "Style" in *Anthropology Today,* ed. A. L. Kroeber. Chicago: University of Chicago Press, 1953. (Reprinted in *Aesthetics Today,* ed. Morris Philipson. New York: Meridian Books, 1961.)

Schlosser, Julius, "Über 'Stilgeschichte' und 'Sprachgeschichte' der bildenden Kunst," *Bayrische Akademie, Sitzungsberichte Phil. Hist. Abt.,* 1935.

Sedlmayr, Hans, *Kunst und Wahrheit.* Hamburg: Rowohlt Taschenbuch Verlag, 1958.

Wellek, René, and Austin Warren, *Theory of Literature.* New York: Harcourt, Brace & Co., Inc., 1949, 1956.

White, John, *Art History and Education.* Hull: University of Hull, 1962.

Wölfflin, Heinrich, *Principles of Art History.* New York: Dover Publications, Inc., 1950, 1956.

INDEX

Archaeology

AERIAL photography, 22-29, 37
Agora of Athens, 60, 61
Alaric, 38-39
American School of Classical
   Studies at Athens, 59-60
Andes, 18, 87
Anthropology, 111-13
Antiquarianism vs. archaeology,
   6-7, 11
Apulia, 26
Archaeology, its scope defined, 5,
   7, 8, 10, 11, 13, 14, 16, 111-21
Archaeometry, 78, 82, 92, 94, 103
Architectural restoration, 55-66
Art history vs. archaeology, 12,
   113-19

BABYLON, 59-60
Baktra, 20
Bass, George, 48
Beazley, John, 117
Belshé, J. C., 104
Blegen, Carl, 42-43
Bradford, Jon, 25, 29, 30
Breasted, James H., 3
Brill, Robert H., 95

CALABRIA, 38, 39
Carbon 14 (*See* Radioactive
   carbon analysis)
Carter, Howard, 20
Central America, 18, 62-64
Ceramic evidence, 42, 43, 44-45,
   67-75, 77, 101-09
Chronological indices, 67-76,
   92-94, 120 (*See also* Dendro-
   chronology, Glass, Radio-
   active carbon analysis,
   Thermoluminescence)
Chronology, relative vs. absolute,
   74-76, 114-15
Coins, restoration of, 51-53
Color in Greek architecture,
   58-59
Conservation of archaeological
   material, 49-55
Cook, R. M., 104
Copan, 62
Corinth, 71
Crete, 36, 120, 121

DENDROCHRONOLOGY, 89, 96,
   97-100
Destruction, types of, 18-20

Western Art History